A Meal For The Road

14 Sermons On The Lord's Supper

Charles E. Link

CSS Publishing Company, Inc.
Lima, Ohio

A MEAL FOR THE ROAD

Copyright © 1994 by
The CSS Publishing Company, Inc.
Lima, Ohio

You may copy the Questions For Reflection Or Group Discussion, pages 85 to 92 if you are the original purchaser, for use as it was intended (worship material for worship use; educational material for classroom use; dramatic material for staging and production). Otherwise all rights reserved. No other part of this publication may be reproduced, stored in a retrieval system, or transmitted in any form or by any means, electronic, mechanical, photocopying, recording, or otherwise, without the prior permission of the publisher. Inquiries should be addressed to: The CSS Publishing Company, Inc., 628 South Main Street, Lima, Ohio 45804.

Scripture quotations are from the *New Revised Standard Version of the Bible,* copyrighted 1989 by the Division of Christian Education of the National Council of the Churches of Christ in the USA. Used by permission.

Scripture quotations are also from the *Revised Standard Version of the Bible,* copyrighted 1946, 1952 (c), 1971, 1973, by the Division of Christian Education of the National Council of the Churches of Christ in the USA. Used by permission.

Library of Congress Cataloging-in-Publication Data

Link, Charles E., 1927–
   A meal for the road : perspectives on the Lord's Supper / by Charles E. Link.
      p.   cm.
   ISBN 1-55673-702-5
   1. Lord's Supper—Sermons. 2. Church year sermons. 3. Sermons, American. I. Title.
BV4257.5.L56   1994
234'.163—dc20   93-30840
                                                                                                         CIP

ISBN 1-55673-702-5   PRINTED IN U.S.A.

To
Martha V. Nipper
who has given three generations
of us an example of Christian living

TABLE OF CONTENTS

Introduction	7
Ruth's Legacy At The Table *Advent*	9
Room At The Table *Christmas*	15
Crumbs From The Table *Epiphany*	21
Foolish Christians *Ash Wednesday*	27
The Gospel In The Supper *Lent*	33
Judas At The Table *Lent*	37
Tangible Signs: Bread And Wine *Maundy Thursday*	43
Pathos And Celebration In The Supper *Maundy Thursday*	49
Prayer At The Supper *Easter or World-wide Communion*	53
A Meal For The Road *Pentecost*	59

People Change With Jesus At The Table *Pentecost*	63
Singing Psalms Of Thanksgiving *Thanksgiving*	69
What We Bring And What We Receive *Confirmation or New Year's Sunday*	75
A New Meal For A New Covenant *First Communion*	81
Questions For Reflection Or Group Discussion	85

INTRODUCTION

One aspect of the early church's vitality was its practice of breaking bread, along with "the Apostles' teaching" and prayer. It was not preaching and prayer with occasional observances of the Lord's Supper. It was the Word experienced along with the Word proclaimed, and prayer as response to the teaching and experiencing of the Word. They remembered their Lord's words as he passed the cup at the Last Supper, "This is the cup of the new covenant [sealed] in my blood." (1 Corinthians 11:25). Word proclaimed, word experienced, and response to the Word as a whole. Through that experience they were instructed and empowered to be Christ's people in the world.

Many Protestant churches today have de-emphasized the Lord's Supper, or lapsed into mechanical, habitual observance. As a result, something in terms of renewal and empowerment has been lost.

The Lord's Supper needs to be constantly interpreted and integrated with the rest of worship. It must again be seen as an indispensable and meaningful event, without which the Christian community is impotent, a pale semblance of the church that "turned the world upside-down" (Acts 17:6) and evidenced that it had "been with Jesus." (Acts 4:13)

It is, then, not an exaggeration to say that attitudes toward the Lord's Supper may be a barometer of a congregation's spiritual vitality or, more positively, that renewed appreciation for the sacrament will accompany the spiritual renewal that churches at this time so ardently seek.

The resurrected Christ was not fully recognized by the Emmaus travelers until "He blessed the bread and broke it." (Luke 24:30) Is it so for his followers today? My conviction is that the answer is yes. And that is why I have written *A Meal For The Road* — Perspectives on the Lord's Supper.

C. E. L.
1993

Advent

RUTH'S LEGACY AT THE TABLE

In the genealogy of Jesus that begins his gospel, Matthew, in good patriarchal style, mentions only the men — except, of course, for Mary, the mother of Jesus, to whom the whole genealogy leads, and Ruth, the great-grandmother of King David, Jesus' most illustrious forebear! Matthew cleverly maintains the male pattern while he introduces the name of Ruth: "... Boaz the father of Obed by Ruth, and Jesse the father of King David." (Matthew 1:5-6) The same ploy is used in culminating the genealogy with the name of Mary, "... and Jacob the father of Joseph the husband of Mary, of whom Jesus was born, who is called the Messiah." (1:16)

Who is this Ruth, and why is she given a place at this illustrious male "table" and our Advent communion table today?

The story that unfolds as one reads the short Old Testament book that bears her name is riveting. It unfolds against the background of hunger and famine. Naomi's husband immigrated to Moab from Judah in search of food and survival for his wife and two sons. In time he died and the sons took Moabite wives, Orpah and Ruth. The tragedy deepened as the sons too died and Naomi saw no alternative but to prepare to return to Judah where, she heard, the drought was waning and a fair harvest had been gleaned. The implication is that the rigorous return journey was taking its toll, for part way on the journey Naomi urged her daughters-in-law to turn around and return to the families of their girlhood, "Go back, each of you, to your mother's house [also widowed?]. May the Lord deal kindly with you, as you have dealt with the dead and with me. The Lord grant that you may find security, each of you in the house of your [new] husband." (Ruth 1:9)

The reaction of the two daughters-in-law is the same, "No, we will return with you to your people." (Ruth 1:10) Tears flowed as Naomi again urged them to seek their own survival by turning back and leaving her to finish the agonizing trip alone. "There is no future for you with me in my barrenness," Naomi responded, "Turn back; go your way . . . the Lord has turned against me." (Ruth 1:13) And it is with that last phrase that we realize the depth of Naomi's despair. Orpah reluctantly, tearfully pulled herself away and turned back. Ruth "clung to her." (1:14)

What follows is a pledge of love and loyalty from Ruth that has become a treasured vow of commitment for several generations, used even at weddings:

> *Do not press me to leave you or to turn back from following you! Where you go, I will go; where you lodge, I will lodge; your people shall be my people, and your God my God. Where you die I will die — there will I be buried. May the Lord do thus and so to me, and more as well, even if death parts me from you!*
> — Ruth 1:16-17, NRSV

Together they made their way back to Bethlehem "at the beginning of the barley harvest." (1:22) At that point another "plot" ensues which results in Ruth's marriage to Boaz, "a prominent rich man" and "kinsman to Naomi on her husband's side." (2:1) It includes a first meal for the two at the edge of a field where Ruth has been picking the bits of grain left behind by the reapers, in accordance with the Law which sought to provide for the needs of poor and hungry people. You see, from the beginning God's concern for the poor was written into the Law of Israel, The understanding was that God's table always had room for the poor and the destitute.

The first meal together of Ruth and Boaz is a simple one of bread and wine at the edge of the field. "Sit here," he said, "and dip your morsel in the sour wine." (Ruth 2:14) From the gracious hand of Boaz, Ruth took the bread and wine, as the disciples were to take the bread and wine from her progeny over 1,000 years hence! The conversation at that outdoor meal centered upon Ruth's selfless pledge to Naomi. Boaz said:

> *All that you have done for your mother-in-law since the death of your husband has been fully told me, and how you left your mother and your native land to come to a people that you did not know before. May the Lord reward you for your deeds and give you refuge under his wings!* — Ruth 2:11-12

It is significant that this blessing comes in the context of a meal of bread and wine. For Boaz' descendant, Jesus, was to bless his disciples with "the peace that passes understanding" at a meal of bread and wine before his betrayal and crucifixion. (John 14:27)

At what was to become known as the last supper, Jesus used an eating occasion to make promises and commitments to his friends that, in the cultural context, were best made with the breaking and passing of bread from a common loaf and the sipping of wine from a common cup.

At that supper, Jesus said, "No one has greater love than this, to lay down one's life for one's friends, [and] you are my friends ..." (John 14:13-14a) To those sitting around the table, the implication that Jesus was prepared to die if it would eliminate the risks for their lives, was unmistakable. And it was sealed by the passing of the bread and the cup!

The similarities of Jesus' pledge to his disciples at the last supper and Ruth's pledge to Naomi as the other daughter-in-law tearfully turned and walked away, are remarkable. Naomi knew that the trip to Bethlehem might never be completed, rigorous as it was and weakened as they were, when she begged Ruth and Orpah to return to Moab. For Ruth to covenant with Naomi to stay by her "for better or worse" might well have been a fatal move for Ruth. There was no guarantee that they would complete the trip nor that they would be able to survive in the new place. Here, indeed, was one of those who would "lay down [her] life for her friend" and thus express the "greatest love" that Jesus could imagine!

That Ruth and Naomi did survive and, more, prosper in the new place was God's response to the kind of selfless commitment that Ruth made and that Jesus' was later to commend in his last supper discourse.

This story and the character Ruth is an excellent place to begin our Advent pilgrimage. Perhaps some here come with Ruth's grief, Orpah's isolation or Naomi's near despair. They suddenly found themselves grieving survivors, hungry and homeless, bereft of the necessities of life, and with uncertain futures. Naomi bewailed the absence of God:

> *The hand of the Lord has turned against me.* — 1:13

> *The Almighty has dealt bitterly with me. I went away full, but the Lord has brought me back empty . . . dealt harshly with me, and . . . has brought calamity upon me.*
> — 1:21

It is hard to think about Christmas when your world is caving in or when your faith is waning. To begin Advent with Ruth, however, is to be reminded that God does not forget any of God's children. Indeed, those who make loving commitments to others will be held up in their resolve by the One who heard the moans of a dying world and sent a child, a descendant of Ruth, to bless and to save.

Christmas reminds us of God's commitment to the human race from the beginning of creation, a commitment marked by grace and truth. In Advent we recognize that we are on the verge of perceiving again the commitment of God to us. For soon the "True Light which enlightens everyone [is] coming into the world" so that "all who receive him, who believe in his name" might have "power to become children of God!"

This is a promise that is sealed for us in a simple meal beside the "threshing floor" — a meal of bread and wine, given with words of blessing: "Peace I leave with you. My peace I give unto you. Not as the world gives, give I unto you. Let not your hearts be troubled. Believe in God, believe also in me." (John 14:1, 27)

Christmas

ROOM AT THE TABLE

One of the treasured pictures we have of Jesus in the gospels is that of him feeding crowds that came to hear him teach in remote places about Galilee. Another is of him socializing at table with people others counted unworthy, "tax collectors and sinners," as the religious people disdainfully called them. (Matthew 9:11) There was always room at Jesus' table for everyone. Not so with the Pharisees, who thought themselves somehow made impure by association with the common people. Who you ate with was a serious matter in that culture, for it implied acceptance, covenant and friendship.

That Jesus found the smugness of the religious elite unacceptable was driven home in his Parable of the Great Banquet where the invited guests failed to appear and replacements were found in "the highways and hedges." (Luke 14:23) It was Jesus' way of saying that there is room for everyone at God's table and that it is to the elite's chagrin that they fail to understand this. It is a failure to understand the impartiality and grace of the God whom they claim to honor and serve.

In light of this major implication of Jesus' ministry, it is ironic to note that when Jesus was born in Bethlehem, there was no room for the Holy Family in the inn. While others partied inside, Joseph and the expectant Mary were relegated to a cow stall out back! Luke suggests that the only people who noticed them and showed hospitality to the new-born child were a few "common people" — the shepherds who had been tending someone's sheep outside the city. We can envision them bringing what dried figs and nuts that they may have carried as provisions for their night-time vigil. The Holy Family's first hosts, then, were humble, common folk, rejected by the religious elite as cavalier in their religious practices.

Sadly, the poor reception that Jesus received at his birth from the majority continued until his crucifixion at their instigation! Not only had he been expelled from their tables but from their synagogues (Luke 4:28-29) and their temple (Luke 22:1-2), as well. The ultimate rejection came when they chose Barabbas over Jesus to be crucified. (Luke 23:18)

The inhospitality did not go unnoticed by Jesus. As would-be followers came to volunteer, Jesus reminded them that "foxes have holes and birds their nests but the Son of Man has no place to rest his head." (Matthew 8:20) And he later warned 70 followers getting set for a missionary journey to anticipate that they may have to expect many inhospitable receptions:

> *Whenever you enter a town and they do not welcome you, go into the streets and say, "Even the dust of your town that clings to our feet, we wipe off in protest against you. Yet know this, the kingdom of God has come near."*
> — Luke 10:10-11

John records the world's inhospitality to Jesus when he writes, "... the world came into being through him; yet the world did not know him. He came to what was his own, and his own people did not accept him." (John 1:10-11) One cannot help but sense the sadness in John's voice as he makes that observation.

Our human perception is that when people experience rejection through life, they become suspicious and, in some cases exhibit anti-social behavior. How many tragic stories have we heard of how rejection in childhood and young adulthood resulted in criminal behavior? Those dealt with inhospitability have, more often than not, become inhospitable themselves, reflecting the behavior of the persons or societies that have rejected or looked down on them.

Not so with Jesus. The narrower his enemy's tables became the broader his became. One contemporary hymn captures this inclusive hospitality of Jesus in a remarkably vivid and artful way:

> *One table spread, throughout the whole wide earth — The King's own feast. From every nation they will come to share, from west to east. Come, all is ready now, our host invites us in. Both bad and good are guests. Let us begin!*[1]

"Both bad and good are guests," and that is what irked the religious elite of Jesus' day. The temptation to judge the "worthiness" of recipients of Jesus' hospitality did not die with the Pharisees. I was saddened a few years back when a young elder, in a church I was serving briefly as interim pastor, came to me after a communion service to say that his experience of communion had been spoiled by an inadequately repentant young woman's partaking of communion a few seats from him. He refused the elements for himself in his irritation with the woman. My response? "You were right not to take communion, feeling as you did. Go home and read Matthew 5:23-24" (i.e. Jesus' teaching about leaving your gift at the altar until you are reconciled with your brother or sister).

Jesus even sat at table with Pharisees! The gospels take special note of this, to be sure. Luke 7:36-50 describes one of these meals in great detail, because it confronts a Pharisee with an "unworthy" woman in a most dramatic way. Jesus not only welcomes the woman to the table but accepts her ministry of footwashing and anointing, to the chagrin of the discourteous host who failed to provide the usual services for a guest.

The contrast between the inclusive Jesus and the exclusive religious person could not be more vivid! Jesus makes the sobering observation, "The [one] who has little to be forgiven has only a little love to give." (Luke 7:47, JBP) The sardonic twist is not to be missed!

It is many miles from the inhospitality of the inn at Bethlehem, the exclusive smugness of the Pharisee, and the world that "received him not" to the Table in the Upper Room! The sacrament of grace, when it is repeated in the spirit and memory of the Master, includes all those who may be blessed by its graces. We have but to recall the words of the master of the great banquet, as Jesus proposes them in his parable, "Whosoever will may come."

The menials, the shepherds, were the first to perceive the breadth and the greatness of this entrance of God's grace in the person of an infant in a cow shed in Bethlehem. They were supposed to be the most receptive when an angel was sent to tell them of the birth of a Savior, a Messiah, a Lord:

> *Do not be afraid; for see — I am bringing you good news of great joy for all the people; to you is born this day in the city of David a Savior, who is the Messiah, the Lord* ...   — Luke 10:11

The rules for the meal were drawn thus to prefer those who could humbly accept their need for the grace of God. The term "the people" is particularly significant in light of the way the superior and self-righteous religious elite used the term. It became a blanket term for all those who could be discounted because they did not share the elite's regard to the Midrash, the Pharisees' voluminous "law about the Law," the fastidious observance of ritual and special days and seasons. When they criticized Jesus they said, disdainfully, "See how the people go out to him." (John 7:12)

To the people's credit, they recognized that Jesus taught with a wondrous authority, "not as the scribes," (Matthew 7:29) and they brought him their sick for their healing and their children for his blessing, and they hung on his words as he taught in village and on hillside.

There is, in many ways, still little hospitality in the world for the inclusive and gracious Jesus. Our society is ripped by division and intolerance. When we come at Christmas to the Table of him whose introduction to the world was an inn in which there was no room, we should recognize that where there is little need in a heart for the forgiveness of God, there is little room for loving others. Let us be moved by the grace and inclusiveness of this Table. We can experience acceptance and forgiveness here and learn the ways of love. "Let us begin!"

---

[1]Hymn *One Table Spread,* Dalton, E. McDonald, ©1972. (The Westminster Press)

Epiphany

CRUMBS FROM THE TABLE

Though we are not told that there were women present at the Last Supper, there are many instances in the gospels where Jesus is pictured with women in connection with a meal. It is at a woman's, Mary's, urgings at a wedding banquet that Jesus performs his first sign: the extending of the wine. We have already written of the "woman of the street" who washed Jesus' feet as he sat at table in Simon the Pharisee's house. We recall, also, the attentiveness of Mary in conversations with Jesus while Martha prepared their evening meal at that Bethany home that became a favorite respite place for Jesus. Mary, momentarily an object of her sister's scorn, was commended by Jesus for "choosing the better part." (Luke 10:42)

One woman who spoke of bread will never be forgotten: the Gentile mother who pled with Jesus to heal her severely epileptic daughter. We can imagine the situation. Wearied in every nerve and fiber of her being by the constant care and oversight her daughter needed, this mother passionately pleaded, "Have mercy on me, O Lord, Son of David." (Matthew 15:22) She didn't grovel but approached him with courage and faith. She heard how he had healed the deaf, the blind, and those with disabling maladies of all kinds. And though she was not a Jew, she had the bravery to believe that Jesus' compassion stretched beyond race or class. All she could think of in that moment was that she might not get the chance again to call upon the healing powers of this godly man.

Jesus' immediate reaction is baffling to us. One scholar concludes that Jesus was having problems understanding who is welcome at God's table, and appears to believe that his primary commission is to his own people. Professor Letty M. Russell says that people like the Gentile mother witnessed to Jesus the need for him to expand his ministry. His response to the woman's pleading? "I was sent only to lost sheep of the house of Israel . . . Let the children be fed first, for it is not fair to take the children's food and give it to the dogs." (Matthew 15:24, 26)

Nowhere else in the gospels do we find Jesus turning away from need as he appears to be doing with this tormented mother. I propose another explanation. Jesus was making an object lesson for the disciples and any other intolerant Jews who might be listening. This was not the only instance in which Jesus had to deal with the prejudice of his people reflected in the attitude of his disciples. A notable instance was when they reacted with amazement when they found him at midday speaking with the Samaritan woman at the well; and not only speaking with her but accepting refreshment from her hand!

Now Jesus is confronted by ethnic prejudice again, and he parodies their own cruel clichés before the pleading woman: "Are we not sent first to the lost sheep of the house of Israel?" and "It is not fitting to take the children's bread and cast it to the dogs" — very uncharacteristic language for Jesus but common prejudicial language for a bigoted Jew or a proud Jewish convert to Christianity.

Hearing their own cruel words coming from the usually compassionate lips of Jesus should have had great impact with those biased Jews standing around. It may seem callous for Jesus to use such an occasion for an object lesson. But I believe it is a compliment to this particular woman. For Jesus seems to have understood that she had the strength, wisdom and instincts to comprehend that from this loving man this was not a test for her but for the others.

She persisted, coming and kneeling before him and saying, "Lord, help me." The very brevity of this entreaty expresses its urgency all the more poignantly. "Lord, see my child as the puppy that eats the crumbs from the master's table..." Yes puppy is the word that she uses rather than dog, reminding Jesus that it is not for herself that she is pleading but for a child of God.

And by that she makes the point (as with Jesus, also for the benefit of those standing by) that every child is God's child and, when stricken like her own, deserving love, no matter what its race or origin.

Lesson time is over, and it is God's love and mercy shining forth from Jesus now. Jesus turns to her and says, "O woman, great is your faith." (Matthew 15:28) In that hour the woman's daughter became the healthy little girl that God wanted her to be.

Jesus was never to use crude, bigoted sayings like those again and, hopefully, neither would his disciples. Yes, God's table is for all people.

Another nameless biblical woman who is presented to us in the context of bread is described only as "the widow of Zarephath." (1 Kings 17:10-17) The land in which she lived had suffered from two years of drought, and she and her hungry son were so desperate that she was gathering bits of straw to boil and eat when Elijah, drawn and weak, stumbled toward her hut.

Fleeing from Jezebel, Elijah had been languishing by a brook and eating what some ravens brought him. The brook now was dry, and Elijah, parched with thirst, made his way to the Gentile widow's house, as God directed him. Elijah knew that God would somehow provide for both his needs and those of the destitute widow and her frail son.

The discouragement of this mother was readily apparent to Elijah. She had managed, somehow, to preserve a handful of meal and a little oil for the inevitable "last meal." How ironic Elijah's request must have seemed to her, "Fetch me some water and make some cakes for me and your son." (1 Kings 17:11) What a test of faith for an anxious and hungry mother!

She perceived Elijah, however, to be a prophet of God. And so, fearfully but hopefully she prepared to feed Elijah from her depleted store. Her hope was not misplaced. She was to find that neither the flask of oil nor the jar of meal would be exhausted as long as the drought lasted. There was enough for a full year — for her son, herself and the prophet! She had "cast her bread upon waters," and it was returning to her.

The widow of Zarephath's hope in the midst of depressing odds was the conduit for this miracle. She had given all that she had when God required it, and because she did not lose hope, God provided bread.

But the drama was not over. Her son had suffered so much from malnutrition that he stopped breathing. For a moment her hope was stretched to its farthest limits. "I am worse off now than before you came," she said to Elijah. "Have you come to carry out a sentence upon me for some past sin?" (1 Kings 17:18) Then, Elijah, who was soon to lay his gift of healing upon his successor, Elisha, again proved God's healing intent. He said with deed what he could never have said so effectively with words: God comes to heal, not to punish. He called upon God to heal the child "while stretching himself upon him." 1 Kings 17:21 says simply, "The child's breath came into him again."

The Gentile woman's hope had been a channel for God's mercy. Then Elijah's words, "See, your son lives," revived her spirit infinitely more than food and drink could ever have. "The word of the Lord in your mouth is truth!" she exclaimed.

Some of us have grown up in traditions that allude to the words of the distraught mother who encountered Jesus, in the confession before communion, "We are not worthy to eat the crumbs under your table." Because of the woman's insight, the confession indicates that no one is worthy and, therefore, all are considered by God to be worthy to be invited to the Lord's banquet.

These stories are but two examples of the dignity accorded to women in the Bible, especially remarkable given the male bias of that culture! There are, indeed, no restrictions on who can be conduit for God's instruction to humankind. God is free to choose anyone to be God's elected messengers to the world. We need to be open, ready to discard cultural and gender chains to hear the most "unlikely" speak to us for God.

And because these women are Gentile women, the lesson deepens. We need to be ready to have the gospel interpreted to us by the outsider, the marginal ones to whom the good news comes with fresh meaning and implications. Not only were the disciples challenged to change by Jesus' mirror to their bigotry, but to find new perspectives on the breadth of God's love and the capacity for faith and understanding from the most "unlikely" sources!

Our calling in Christ before the foundation of the earth (Ephesians 1:1-14) is for the purpose of letting the whole world know about the welcomeness at God's Table. The church is not a new Israel, a holy assembly set apart to the Lord, but the beginning of a new humankind called to exhibit the new belongingness offered to all.

It is with purpose that Jesus in his Parable of the Great Banquet (Matthew 22:1-14) pictures the master sending his servants out into the highways and hedges and inviting everyone they could find to the wedding banquet. There is plenty of room at God's table for all whom God loves!

Ash Wednesday

FOOLISH CHRISTIANS

Let me tell you about the late Japanese evangelist Toyohiko Kagawa, by the world's standards one of the greatest of misfits! He turned his back on a privileged life in a Buddhist home to become a Christian evangelist among the poor and disreputable in the slums of Tokyo. He made his mark, for though legally blind in mid-life, Kagawa was as well known as E. Stanley Jones or Frank Laubach. He displayed qualities of both, plus the eastern mind's ability to plumb the mystical and spiritual depths. His written meditations are still among the finest.

The dark side of all this is that when Kagawa turned his back on his reputable Buddhist ancestry, he became an embarrassment, and his timing, in terms of American war sentiment, made him unacceptable here. So he became a man without a country — a misfit, an anachronism!

But Kagawa's trials, his experience of human rejection, gave him empathy with the Paul of 1 Corinthians 1:17-19, and he reflected:

> *A foolish Christian! The laughingstock of the world! I have spent half of my lifespan as a foolish Christian.*

All sorts of so-called worldly pleasures have slipped away from me. I have spent half my life in a state describable as being tied to a garbage can. Despised as a narrow-minded man and looked down upon as a stubborn man, I have spent much of each day for half a lifetime in tears.

When I was forced to take my stand at the foot of the cross, summoned from a prideful, materialistic environment, my people labeled me as a hypocrite, a member of a gang of traitors and heathens. Even among my fellow Christians I am not always welcome. I am excluded as a heretic, a socialist, a flippant man, destitute of profound thoughts.[1]

How like Paul's description of his condition after his conversion on the Damascus Road! Before that, Paul was a successful young Pharisee, secure and upwardly mobile. Of his life after his conversion, Paul says:

In toil and hardship, through many a sleepless night, in hunger and exposure, and, furthermore, in constant anxiety over the state of these many churches.
— 2 Corinthians 11:27-28

What kind of a result is that for people who have given so much?

But then we recall that it was not different for Jesus. His life was as exemplary as we can imagine: faithful, obedient, and self-sacrificing. However, he was not a success in the usual sense of that word. To family and friends, he, too was a misfit and an embarrassment. Jesus did not make his mark in life but in suffering and death! For despite his powerful teaching and deeds, he appeared weak and defenseless. People criticized him. He was ridiculed and mocked. And his "kingship" was caricatured with a crown of thorns and a purple robe. A cycnical sign was hung: "Here is your King of the Jews!" (Matthew 27:37)

In those last hours, from the point of view of those who passed by deriding him and the religious leaders who mocked him, Jesus looked every bit of a failure! It is reported that his closest friends were ashamed: one betrayed him, another denied him, others ran for cover, and his enemies gloated.

As someone has rightly pointed out, any institution or religion astute in public relations would have concealed such facts about their founder. This is certainly not the way to make followers and influence people! But, to the contrary, the gospels document in great detail the insane contradictions in Jesus' life and way. Even Paul, that exemplary church organizer, proclaimed the embarrassment of Jesus' ill-fittingness:

> *For [while] the word of the cross is folly to those who are perishing . . . it pleased God through the folly of what we preach to save those who believe . . . God chose what is foolish in the world's eyes to shame the wise, what is weak to shame what is strong.*
> — 2 Corinthians 1:18-27

We're told that in medieval times there was a holiday that bears some similarities to our contemporary Lenten Eve Mardi Gras. It was called Fools' Feast. Apparently, on that day, parish priests and ordinarily serious villagers put on outrageous masks, sang off-color songs, and kept everyone awake with their hilarity! Bottom-rung clergy adorned themselves in the regalia of bishops and paraded the ceremony of church and palace. Victor Hugo in *The Hunchback of Notre Dame* pictured the pitiable Quasimodo being ceremoniously crowned as Fools' Pope during a Fools' Feast.

We might guess that Jesus' mother, Mary, would have been greatly amused by such a day. For Mary envisioned the Lord putting down "the mighty from their thrones and exalt[ing] those of low degree!" (Luke 1:52)

One historian says of the Fools' Feast that it was a greatly different kind of world on that one day — one where the least were first and accepted values were turned around. Fools became kings and choirboys prelates. An upside-down world where the unexpected happens was celebrated at Fools' Feast.

The Lord's Supper could be called a Fools' Feast. For here we celebrate and announce the reversal of the world's values. The honored host served and washed feet! We remember when we take the bread and wine how Jesus' greatest victory was won in death. We remember that his death was not the end but, in many important ways, a beginning! Jesus would have the "last laugh."

It must seem odd to the world that we call a day full of anguish "Good Friday." We do it because we perceive what looks like a defeat becoming a phenomenal victory! We know that we have gotten to Easter Sunday by passing through a "dark" Friday, so we call it "good."

The world was longing for God to come powerfully and make things right. However God came in weakness and agony to submit to death on a cross. That is how God gets mankind on track again! That's something the world has a hard time understanding, for it is contrary to the way things usually get done. But God's ways are above our ways, and God's weakness and foolishness are greater than our so-called wisdom and strength. (1 Corinthians 3:19)

It is a pattern that we see repeated in our own day. We remember how Soviet Communists wrote off celebrated physicist Andrew Sahkarov as a misfit when he defected to the west in protest of their view of the world as an abstraction, the worship of power, and the attempt to reshape life. "I find it hard to imagine the universe and human life without some guiding principle, without a source of spiritual 'warmth' that is nonmaterial and unbound by physical laws, he wrote in his *Memoirs*. Ironically, this misfit's articles were later featured in *Science and Religion* (to the chagrin of the late Khrushchev, who founded it in 1959 as part of his virulent campaign against religion)!

There is no question that could have come, predictably, in power and strength to defeat injustice and evil. Instead, God invites humanity to a table of reconciliation, a dinner for misfits. "Both bad and good are guests," says one contemporary communion hymn.

No one, surely, would criticize God for considering us rebels and outlaws. But God chose not to do that. God opens this Table to all who will rashly follow Jesus, one who was "despised and rejected of man." (Isaiah 53:3) And behold, we are no longer outlaws. God reaches out to us in compassion and grace, changing us into "heirs of God, joint-heirs with Christ, if so be that we suffer with him." (Romans 8:17)

When we partake of what is sometimes called the Eucharist, from the Greek *eucharistia,* meaning "gratitude," we remember with thanks what God has done for us in happy anticipation of God's promises to all people. Communion is an oath of allegiance to God's reign. Eating the bread and drinking the cup from Jesus' hand means giving ourselves to his "foolish" ways. It means laying our lives on the line as a thankful offering of ourselves to God. This we do, even if it looks crazy to the rest of the world. "We are fools for Christ's sake," said Paul. (1 Corinthians 4:10)

Many might ask who in their right mind would choose to follow a king who washes the feet of those who will "turn tail" when he is arrested? What people with "all their marbles" would want to take seriously the contrary ethics of Jesus: walking the second mile, turning the other cheek, loving enemies, and embracing the role of servant?

Such radical choices face us when we come to the Lord's Table. But God helps us to choose the Jesus way of life and belief, with all its risks and costs. No matter who we have been or how we have been behaving, Jesus, unexplainably, persists in reaching out to us. The Lord's Supper is a time to celebrate the life that God poured out in love for our sake, a life that calls for similar reckless sacrifice from us.

After enduring what he did as a Japanese Christian renegade unacceptable on both sides of the globe, Kagawa wrote:

> *All that does not matter in the least, I am a captive of Christ. I am a slave of the cross. I belong among the foolish. In other words, I have just taken off on a journey to the Holy Mountain, stark naked, throwing all earthly*

things away. If it appears foolish to the eyes of other people, I can't help it.[2]

It makes sense to avoid ridicule, but it is not Christ's way. With him we do not ignore or escape what other faithful endure. But we move, like Kagawa, toward the kingdom of God. Only then do we live in confidence of a completed kingdom. As we break bread and drink the cup, we recall and celebrate Jesus' broken body and shed blood. And more: in hope we proclaim, "Christ has died! Christ has risen! Christ will come again!"

Perhaps some will want to claim the benefits of that vision without following Jesus' suffering in this life. They will miss the assurance that the Table is able to give of a completed kingdom, even as it empowers us to face the mockery, injustice and suffering that accompanies walking with the servant of all.

Our confidence in God's emerging kingdom gives us the capacity to endure the hardships of being "a foolish Christian."

So the Lord's Supper is a solemn and joyous feast for misfits who are waiting for the miracle of being transformed into children of God.

---

[1]Kagawa, *Meditations* (Harper & Bros.) 1950, Med. No. 8.

[2]*Ibid.*

Lent

THE GOSPEL IN THE SUPPER

John Calvin said that the true church is where the gospel is faithfully preached and the sacraments faithfully administered. This was in an age when the Western Church had come to think of itself in many more complex and political ways. The church, it was said, is wherever allegiance is given to Peter's successor in Rome; wherever daily mass is said by priests in the apostolic succession; and where adherents practice many rules and observances. The church for them was a power-broker, defining kingdoms and crowning monarchs.

Luther recognized, through his study of the New Testament, that what was meant to be a servant-church had become the master and political church, and that the gospel in all its simplicity, had been obscured in the process. He set out, against all odds, to preach again salvation by grace through faith.

Jesus anticipated that the gospel, born of atoning sacrifice and suffering service, might be obscured by future generations, so he encased it in a sacrament that he mandated should be repeated often "in remembrance" of him. The bread was to be for us his "body broken," and the wine his "blood shed." How simple and yet how profound. "As by one man's disobedience many were made sinners, so by one man's obedience many shall be saved," Paul was later to write, using an analogy that we can all comprehend. (Romans 5:19) That, in its simplest form, is the gospel!

Even during Paul's lifetime it apparently began to be lost. "Some preach Christ out of rivalry," Paul observed, (Philippians 1:17) meaning that for some preachers the desire to outshine other preachers became more important than the proclamation. And that was happening within a generation of Jesus' atoning death!

What are some of the "passionless" gospels that are being preached in our own generation? They include the gospels of personal poise and prosperity — popular psychology beefed up with biblical references; telling us how to be greedy without feeling guilty, and that there's nothing wrong with a lifestyle that puts "me first."

It is more than coincidence that in the mega-churches and pseudo-churches of cable television, where such themes are presented, the sacrament of communion is rarely mentioned or observed. What do you do with a gospel that bespeaks a body broken for us and blood shed for us; that calls for death to self and new life in a Savior with nail prints on his hands? What do you do with a Savior who calls for his followers to take up their crosses and follow him, (Matthew 16:24) and who says that he who seeks his life will lose it? (Matthew 10:39)

A short time ago an article appeared in a denominational magazine that purported to define a gospel that embraces the best aspects of liberalism, fundamentalism, ecumenism, conservativism, etc. But in the process of describing "what Reformed theology is all about," the clergy author made barely any reference to the cross and only a passing reference to Savior and salvation. We are told that Christ died "but" was raised, as if the only value of the cross is to set the stage for Jesus' resurrection. In other words, in his eagerness to move to the celebrative aspects of the Christian life, the writer has made a postscript of the apex of our Lord's obedience, his redemptive submission to death on a cross. It is no coincidence that this purported summary of Reformed theology included no reference at all to the sacraments. The words of institution of the Supper — "body broken," "blood shed," "covenant sealed in my blood" — are difficult to blend with a gospel that bypasses the cross on its path from Christmas to Easter and Pentecost.

Emil Brunner, late Swiss Reformed theologian, in public lecture in 1955, stressed how critical the crucifixion is for the gospel to be the gospel. "God goes to a cross and tells us that we may leave our sins there. The cross reveals the breadth of God's love and the depth of our waywardness," he said.

Brunner went on to say that at the foot of the cross you and I can be freed from the tentacles of a guilty past. In the context of Paul's words about Jesus' redemptive obedience, I understand this to mean that the ultimate Judge tells me that when Jesus stands with me at the place of assize, his merits attach to me and more than make up for the ways I've disappointed the God of high hopes. Now I am judged not on my own record but on Christ's, to whose hand I cling. He was as obedient as I was disobedient, and God is willing to attribute Jesus' merits to me. "God annuls our past in order to free us from its guilty burden and give us true presence in his love. That is what the cross achieves for us," Brunner said.

Another 20th century theologian, Dietrich Bonhoeffer, martyred for his faith, warned against a "cheap grace." That is, a gospel that ignores Jesus' cross and ours; one that welcomes the fruits of salvation without understanding and appreciating the redemptive obedience demonstrated by Christ and the suffering service to which he calls us today. That may not be a message that readily attracts the masses, but it is the gospel of the cross. Paul resolved "to preach nothing ... except Jesus Christ, and him crucified," though it was "a stumbling block to the Jews and folly to Gentiles." (1 Corinthians 2:2, 1:23)

Yes, there is a new covenant centered in grace, not law. Responding to it, embracing it, does indeed elicit praise, but we must never forget that it is, as Jesus said at the Last Supper, a covenant "sealed in my blood." (Matthew 26:28)

Alan Paton has a character in one of his South African novels say as he is about to enter heaven, "I hate the thought that I might come to some final judgment and be asked 'Where are your wounds?' and have nothing to show." We don't do Christians today a favor by presenting Christ without his cross and a Christian life that gets us to Easter and Pentecost without calling us to travel the Via Dolorosa.

In some churches there is the practice of asking those assembled for communion to hold the small glass of juice in their hands until everyone has received, and then partake together "as a sign of our unity in Christ." Have you ever noticed how the tiny glass of red liquid pulsates with every beat of your heart? For me it becomes a moment to contemplate the heart of Jesus that beats through my heart. This is one of the true miracles of being "in Christ," as Paul puts it. (Colossians 1:27) His life continues, in part, in my life — "joint heirs with Christ, if indeed we suffer with him." (Romans 8:17) It reminds me, also, of the cost of my salvation.

The Lord's Supper words of institution militate against a euphoric gospel that downplays the suffering that was endured for us and the suffering service "to the least of these" to which we are called in Matthew 25.

A eucharistic prayer of thanksgiving from the old *Presbyterian Book of Common Worship* speaks of Jesus who "took our nature upon him, to suffer death upon the cross for our redemption," making "a full, perfect, and sufficient sacrifice for the sins of the whole world." It calls upon us "to present ourselves ... to be a reasonable, holy, and living sacrifice."

These are the themes that will never be lost as long as we are truly "present" at the Table of our Lord and hear again his words, "Take, eat; this is my body broken for you," and "This is the cup of the new covenant sealed in my blood. Drink of it, all of you." (Matthew 26:26-28)

Lent

JUDAS AT THE TABLE

Where did it begin — Judas' disillusionment with Jesus? The gospels give only a few subtle clues. Perhaps he was there when John the Baptist's disciples came with John's question, "Are you he who is to come, or shall we look for another?" (Matthew 11:3) expressing John's wavering certainty that Jesus was the Messiah come to "clear the threshing floor, gather his wheat ... [and] burn the chaff with unquenchable fire." (Matthew 3:12)

If Iscariot, as some scholars have suggested, is less an indication of where Judas was from as it is that he was a member of the revolutionary faction called Sicarius or "dagger men," we have an indication of where Judas' sentiments lay. He would welcome a Messiah who would overthrow the colonial power and make Israel a nation to reckon with again. Jesus, by contrast, seemed almost indifferent to the Roman oppression, and even urged his followers to "pray for those who persecute you" and "resist not those who are evil." He urged them to "go two miles with him who forces you to go one," a clear reference to the right of Roman military to press subject people into service within their rules of occupation. (Matthew 5:44, 41)

To be sure, John and Judas were becoming disillusioned with Jesus for quite different reasons. John wanted Jesus to concentrate on a call to repentance and the ushering in of the Day of the Lord, a day of reckoning and judgment. Judas probably wanted Jesus to use his charisma with the masses to foment a successful revolt and overthrow the Roman overlords. Perhaps he felt at the start that God had sent Jesus specifically for this purpose. Jesus was, after all, of the lineage of David, the last great warrior king.

But, beyond inference, there are more direct clues to Judas' growing disillusionment with Jesus. He was guardian of the purse for the disciples and, as such, was involved in discussions about the appropriate use of funds. Most certainly he was the one who, before the miraculous feeding of the multitude as reported in Luke, said to Jesus, "Surely you're not implying that we should buy food for all these people!" (Luke 9:13)

Similarly, at the Pharisee's house when the prostitute anointed Jesus' feet with costly ointment, it was Judas who objected, saying, "Why was not this ointment sold for 200 denarii and given to the poor?" (John 12:5) John cannot resist offering a parenthetical comment: "This he said, not that he cared for the poor but because he used to take from the money box what he needed for himself." (John 12:6) More than that, it illustrates a growing contentiousness with Jesus, a pickiness that was symptomatic of a critical attitude toward Jesus and a growing disappointment with the character of Jesus' mission.

Judas' wavering faith in the direction Jesus' ministry was taking most certainly made him a ploy for Jesus' enemies among the religious establishment, as well as for Jesus' old enemy, the Dark Tempter who first confronted Jesus in the wilderness. (4:1-11) Then, Luke comments, "The devil departed from him until an opportune time." (Luke 4:13) Judas' wavering faith in Jesus provided that more "opportune time!"

Jesus acknowledged Judas' treacherous conspiracy with the priests before he broke the bread and shared the cup the night of the Last Supper. Who would not have understood if Jesus had chosen to expel Judas before the institution of that sacred meal? Matthew and Mark, however, suggest the opposite. The prediction of betrayal just precedes the meal, and there is no indication that Judas was left. Luke places the prediction after the Lord's Supper, with the very clear implication that Judas was there the full time. John is apparently scandalized that Judas should have joined in the Supper and provides a situation where "after he ate the morsel [of bread], Satan entered into him." (John 13:27a)

The significance of Judas' inclusion in the partaking of the Last Supper cannot, I believe, be overestimated! The human question of worthiness is a serious one for us. Paul even gave it a paragraph in one of his epistles: "Whoever eats the bread or drinks the cup in an unworthy manner will be guilty of profaning the body and blood of the Lord." (1 Corinthians 11:27) Of course, the context there is people coming for the feast that follows, with no preparation or contemplation given to the significance of "discerning the body." (1 Corinthians 11:29)

The words of invitation that ordinarily precede the communion service itself are deliberately phrased in such a way so as not to imply that we come to the Table on our own worthiness. We come not on our own worthiness but upon the worthiness of "The Son of Man who came . . . to give his life a ransom for many." (Matthew 20:28)

There may be legitimate reasons for not partaking of the Lord's Supper in terms of our own lack of attitudinal preparation, such as that spelled out by Jesus in Matthew 5:23, 25 — "If you are offering your gift at the altar, and there remember that your brother has something against you . . . go, be reconciled to your brother, and then come and offer your gift" — but righteousness cannot be one of them! Ours is a borrowed righteousness. Jesus had no trouble pointing out the flaws of those religious leaders who considered themselves righteous, and looked down on others as sinners! If in doubt, read again his parable of the Pharisee and the Publican in Luke 18, where the situation again is worship.

The irony is that the factor that made Judas welcome at the Table was the same one that caused him to fall out with Jesus: the gospel of grace. This theme dominated the teaching and way of Jesus increasingly as his ministry progressed. It was the message of grace that caused the people in the Nazareth synagogue to react hostilely and violently. For Jesus did something that a nationalistic messiah would never do — he cited God's love for the Gentiles!

The theme of God's grace extended to "outsiders" was illustrated again when Jesus healed the particularly dear slave of the centurion. (Luke 7:1-10) We can hear Judas saying, "Surely our faith makes us worthy to receive God's special favors." But, instead, he saw Jesus exhibiting a shockingly lavish grace extended to Phoenician widows, Syrian generals, Roman centurions and even those, like Judas, who resent the grace of God toward all. Judas wanted Jesus to exhibit the authority of a military and political messiah; instead, Jesus exercised his authority on the basis of grace.

Judas' inclusion at the Last Supper is proof that Jesus had not written him off, had not given up on him. He recalled Judas' earlier enthusiasm and energy. Jesus would have known about Judas' affiliation with the Sicarius, but he took a calculated risk and appointed him treasurer of their meager funds, perhaps in the hope that Judas would mature best in an atmosphere of trust and confidence rather than of suspicion. When Jesus reproved him, as he did at Simon the Pharisee's house, it was with gentleness and patience.

Judas' change of heart is tragically evident in his actions following the arrest of Jesus. "When Judas saw that [Jesus] was condemned, he repented and brought back the 30 pieces of silver to the chief priests, saying, 'I have sinned against innocent blood' ... and he went and hanged himself." (Matthew 27:3-5) How much anguish is packed into those few deceptively simple words! Judas' remorse was the deepest that can be experienced.

The Lord's Supper is a meal of God's grace. And as it included Judas, it can certainly include those of us who have been brought up short again and again on our potential to betray, to contradict by our actions and attitudes the values we profess, to try to shape Jesus by our mold, instead of being molded by his life in ours.

Thank God the meal is not an award for being good but a treatment for those who need grace! Thank God the meal is not about our righteousness but about God's forgiveness!

In a particularly dark period in my ministry, I found good reason for partaking of the bread and the cup with passionate understanding and appreciation. I had — not with malice of forethought but in clumsy defense of a young colleague — revealed what had been shared with me in confidence, to a person who's anger at the young pastor I had failed to adequately measure. The results were disastrous. Understandably, the young pastor was angry and inconsolable. He resigned. I lost the respect of many of our associates. My own career was significantly effected. My efforts at repentance and restitution were, for the most part, fruitless. All I could think of was that I had betrayed a brother. I rehearsed the tragic incident over and over again in my mind for many a sleepless night, wondering how I could have been so naive, so careless. I had not only failed my friend but myself. I had failed my Lord.

But then I came to the Lord's Table, remembering from years before the carved wood relief of the Last Supper in the seminary chapel. Not only was John, the "beloved disciple," there, as Da Vinci originally portrayed it, but so was Peter who would soon deny him, Thomas who would soon doubt him, and Judas who would soon betray him. And, slowly, I came to understand that I am welcome at this blessed Table, not because of my worthiness or righteousness but because of God's goodness and God's grace as shown to me in Jesus Christ.

I don't have to move into the future dragging the guilt and regret of past failings. I can leave my sins at the foot of the cross and draw on Jesus' Spirit as I move out in hope. That is what the Supper does for me. That is what it can do for you!

"I will not drink again of this fruit of the vine, [John, Peter, Thomas . . . yes, Judas,] until I drink it new with you in my Father's kingdom." (Matthew 26:29)

Maundy Thursday

TANGIBLE SIGNS: BREAD AND WINE

Step back with me to the Upper Room the night of the Last Supper. Jesus reintroduces a subject that he broached a week earlier when he set his face steadfastly toward Jerusalem, telling his disciples then that he must "undergo great suffering and be killed and on the third day be raised." (Matthew 16:21, NRSV) Peter then raged at him saying, "God forbid it, Lord! This must never happen to you." (v. 22)

Now, on this eve of the Passover, Jesus introduces the dark subject again, "I'm not going to be with you much longer. Don't try to follow me. Where I am going you cannot come ... But you will still have one another, so it's more important than ever that you love one another, just like I have loved you." (John 13:33-34, author's paraphrase)

It is in this context that this rush of questions comes from the disciples. Ignoring his admonition to love one another, they ask, "Where are you going?" "Why can't we follow you?" "Lord, we do not know where you are going; how can we know the way?" and "Will you leave us without showing us the Father?" (John 31:36, 14:5, 8, author's paraphrase) Jesus, who is used to hearing unspoken words behind outward questions, knows that what the disciples are really saying is, "Don't leave us! We are nothing without you." — Sure, there was Jesus' promise about a Spirit's coming, "He will teach you everything." (John 14:26, NRSV) But it will not be the same. Who can see or touch a Spirit?

Suddenly, this incident makes us aware of how much Jesus' actual physical presence, quite aside from his marvelous spirituality, had meant to those men who had, almost three years before, turned their backs on their jobs and families, the lives they were living, left all their securities and followed him.

Now recollections of their dependence upon him came flooding in upon them. When they had failed to minister with power in the healing and helping of people, he had, more than once, stepped in to rescue the situation. When they were baffled about how to feed and care for the multitudes who often followed him hither and yon, he stepped in and saved the day. When they were confused and in disagreement about the character of the kingdom and their place in it, he set them right with his divine and penetrating insights about humility and service. When they were argued into a corner and made to feel guilty by the devious and clever scribes and Pharisees, his words like a rapier cut the learned teachers down to size and sent them packing. When they were dried up and depleted in spirit, he would call them to a place apart and pray with them and for them, and they would find new energy and new inspiration. When a storm on a lake or in life would fill them with terror and dismay, he would rise in the boat or approach them on the turbulent waters, and their hearts would be suddenly calmed and the terror dispelled.

But now this face, this voice, these hands and feet were not going to be around any more. "I am not going to be with you much longer; don't try to follow me; where I am going you cannot come" were the dark words.

Yes, behind the intellectual, surface questions — "We do not know where you are going; how can we know the way," and "Will you leave us without showing us the Father?" is the real exclamation, really a groan, "Lord, don't leave us!

We need your proddings, your gestures, your prayers, your words, your smiles, your hugs, your warmth, your love. Where shall we be without them?"

Jesus' preliminary answers make good sense: "I'll send you the Spirit, an Advocate, to teach you everything. And I'll leave you one another. Furthermore, if you love each other as I have loved you, you'll never be alone or lonely." (John 14:26, 13:34, author's paraphrase)

"We hear that, Lord. Thank you. But it is you we'll miss! We are nothing without you, as we were nothing before you came. Having you at our side has made all the difference!"

Can you crawl into their skins and understand just a little of what those despondent disciples were feeling on the night of his announcement, "These are our last hours together; don't try to follow me; where I am going you cannot come"?

But Jesus, understanding and being so completely sympathetic with human nature after those 30 years walking with us, does something in the manner of God from earliest times. Do you remember how much trouble Moses had convincing the people of Israel of God's true presence and availability? Moses knew that the people needed something tangible, if they were not to lapse into idolatry, to stand for God's presence with them as they moved through the wilderness on their way to the promised land. And the God who had reluctantly provided a name "Yahweh" (meaning "I am" — an ironic answer that implied "My presence should be enough"), that God provided them with an ark, a chest, to hold the Tablets of Law. That sacred chest was carried with them when they moved from one place to another, and it rested in a tent or tabernacle when they pitched camp. It had the effect of evidencing to them that the God who graciously made covenant with them, who chose them, would not forsake them, "God is with you. He that keepeth Israel will neither slumber nor sleep. He shall be thy keeper, thy shade upon thy right hand. The Lord of Hosts is with us. The God of Jacob is our refuge." (Psalm 121:2-3, 46:11, KJV)

And now God was, in Jesus, to condescend to the human need for tangible signs again. Jesus took what was at hand — a cup of wine and some bread — and he said, "These shall be to you my body and my blood. You shall frequently receive them together recalling these words of mine, and your memory of me shall then become an actual experience of my presence." (1 Corinthians 11:24-25, author's paraphrase)

You know, the Reformers reacted against the Roman Catholic doctrine of transubstantiation that said that the elements of bread and wine, though unchanged in actual appearance, became, upon the words of consecration, the actual body and blood of Jesus. Luther and Calvin rejected this as so much "hocus-pocus," but at the same time they knew that there was a unique experience of the actual presence of Christ in the act of communion, and they urged its observance at least every Lord's Day. For that is how Christ means to reassure us. So we, too, they insisted, may speak about the real presence of Christ in this simple act of coming to Christ's table and communing with him and with one another, that is, in the total act of communion.

There was an experiment by Emerson and other so-called "transcendentalists" in colonial America. They said that human beings could become so elevated in their thinking that they could be baptized without water and take communion without bread and wine. A noble idea. Fact is, their movement to a higher spirituality was short-lived and is little remembered, so faulty was their understanding of human nature.

American hostage Terry Anderson, when in captivity in Lebanon, became a father. Asked where her daddy was, his little girl would point to a picture on the mantle, "There is my daddy." You see, until he came walking back into their lives, that precious picture said it all: the warmth, good humor, affection and love in his face, caught by the camera. Until he came walking off that plane and took her up in his arms, that picture stayed glued to the mantle! It was her one tangible link to her father until he came.

That is not too far off as an analogy to communion. For Jesus had further words that evening. After giving them this sacrament as evidence of his continuing love and life, he said, "I will never again drink of the fruit of the vine until I drink it new with you in the kingdom of God." (Mark 14:25, NRSV) Communion is a precious interim sacrament that will be supplanted by our reunion with Jesus in the fulfilled kingdom of God. That is a certainty based upon the promise of Jesus — our assurance and our hope!

Six hundred years before Christ, Jeremiah had a marvelous premonition of a new covenant life that would need no tangible signs but only the reality of God's presence:

> *I will put my law within them, says the Lord. I will write it on their hearts; and I will be their God, and they shall be my people . . . they shall all know me, from the least of them to the greatest.*   — 31:33-34, NRSV

Until then, take, eat; this is Christ's body. Drink ye all of it; this is Christ's blood. (after 1 Corinthians 11:24-25)

Maundy Thursday

PATHOS AND CELEBRATION IN THE SUPPER

Artists will tell you that the process of sculpting, painting or carving a major piece includes deep elements of agony and ecstasy, even as Irving Stone pictured it for Michelangelo in his painting of the unprecedented murals for the Sistine Chapel ceiling. It begins with the excitement of anticipation, as the concept emerges in your imagination. The pristine tools and surfaces fairly cry out for the artist's caress and exploration. It continues through the tedious work of the half-way process, when the forms are but awkward and faint promises of what they shall be; when the beginning excitement has faded, and self doubts begin to plague you.

At that mid-point many artists admit to abandoning or destroying the project and moving to something else. Who has not wondered how Da Vinci would have completed his "Virgin, St. John and Jesus" or Schubert his eighth symphony? But sometimes the artist recognizes this is a necessary part of the creative process and perseveres. With several more determined strokes of the brush or chisel, the prospect of completion and joyous achievement emerges! Is there any ecstasy greater than that when the artist finally sets down his or her tools and backs up for the last time, to get an overview of the work that was once only a tantalizing possibility in his or her mind?

It is easy to make an analogy, I think, from this to the rest of life. The times we will remember with the greatest clarity and impact are those that plumbed the depths, endured the transitions, and explored the heights of human striving, experience and relationships.

That is why the Lord's Supper is so tantalizing for us. Even the traditional names for it hint at its dual aspects. *Eucharistia,* a Greek word meaning thanksgiving, lifts up for us the celebrative side of the Supper. Jesus blessed the meal with a prayer of thanksgiving to God, for Paul reports, "When he had given thanks, he broke it and said . . ." (1 Corinthians 11:24) The Words of Institution begin with words of thanksgiving.

The thanksgiving element is further underscored by the fact that the Supper is set by the Synoptic Gospels in the context of a Passover celebration. "Where will you have us prepare for you to eat the Passover?" the disciples ask Jesus. (Matthew 26:17)

The Passover was not a somber but a joyous occasion, recalling the deliverance from the "Angel of Death" just prior to the liberation from Egypt, by the required lamb's blood on the doorposts. It included singing and thankful recollection of the events of the exodus. The Lord's Supper is sometimes called "The Christian Passover," recalling the liberation from sin and death that God's Lamb, Jesus, accomplished in his sacrificial life, death, and resurrection. The "Long Prayer" in the traditional order for communion is a grand prayer of thanksgiving to God for the redemption found in Christ and his cross, and for the new life that it offers.

But at the same time that we perceive the original Supper's joyous side, we are aware of its somber and ominous aspects. For Paul reported, "The Lord Jesus on the same night in which he was betrayed took bread . . ." (1 Corinthians 11:23) What began in a celebrative mood for the road-weary disciples soon took on dark overtones, as Jesus announced his imminent betrayal, (Mark 14:18) his approaching crucifixion (Luke 22:37) and Peter's forthcoming denial. (John 13:38) The situation was made more tense by the disciples' argument over "who would be greatest," (Luke 22:24) and the refusal of any one of them to perform the humble service of footwashing for the others, as would be expected before the eating began. (John 13:5) Jesus' first words, as they took their places around the traditional meal, warmed their hearts, "I have earnestly desired to eat this Passover with you...." (Luke 22:15a) We can imagine their nods as he spoke. We can picture them saying, "Yes, Jesus, we feel the same way. This has been a busy and trying week for us: that turmoil in the temple court, the endless debates with the scribes and temple leaders, and the pressing and needy crowds. There's been no let-up at all; no time to ourselves." Any illusion they had of "a family home evening" was soon shattered with Jesus' next ominous words, "... before I suffer ...," (Luke 22:15b) reintroducing a theme they had hoped they had merely dreamed some time earlier, "The Son of Man will be handed over to the Gentiles; he will be mocked and insulted, and spat upon ... and killed ..." (Luke 18:32) The somberness of that prediction had faded amidst the spontaneous accolades of the crowds as he entered the walled city a short time later, a demonstration that alarmed the temple leaders. "Order your disciples to stop," they commanded. (Luke 19:39)

But in a moment during this last night together, they heard Jesus' reference to his impending suffering and death, and what was assumed to be a joyous feast threatened to become a somber vigil.

Those disciples had, after all, but a few years with Jesus of Nazareth — a small fraction of each of their lives, but the most momentous part because it plumbed the depths and scaled the heights, from swamped boats and sleepless night-time prayer vigils to a mountaintop transfiguration, a triumphant preaching mission, and a "Palm Sunday" accolade.

Like us, their most memorable experiences and relationships were not those where they coasted through some bog of mediocrity, but those that involved struggle and success, trial and victory — the depths and the heights — as the Last Supper did and as communion does!

"I will not drink again of the fruit of the vine until I drink it new with you in the kingdom of God," said Jesus. (Matthew 26:29) And with those simple words the somber mood was broken. "Every time we eat this bread and drink this cup we show forth the Lord's death until he comes," Paul declares (1 Corinthians 11:26) reminding us that the sadness of the Supper is not the last word. There is the promise of victory!

It is easy on Maundy Thursday to exaggerate the element of pathos in the Lord's Supper. There was the shallowness of Palm Sunday's praise. The voices soon turned to derision, and they would eventually call for Jesus' death and the release of Barabbas. "O Sacred Head, now wounded; with grief and shame weighed down..." But Jesus on that night did not let the emerging shadow of the cross keep him from painting a picture of an inevitable victory: "I will eat and drink again with you in my Father's kingdom." That lifted them, and it lifts us, from despair into hopeful anticipation!

Both elements were at the Lord's Supper. And they remain there today in the sacrament of communion, recalling Jesus' promise that struggle will give way to victory when he banquets with us in the fulfilled kingdom of God. Come, Lord Jesus, come! Amen.

Easter or World-wide Communion Sunday

PRAYER AT THE SUPPER

When the resurrected Christ sat at table with the two discouraged followers at the roadside inn outside Emmaus, he took the bread in his hands and, in a characteristic way that they recognized, gave thanks to God.

We can only guess what he said and how he said it. A traditional Jewish grace would have begun, perhaps with the *Shema:*

> *Hear, O Israel, the Lord thy God is one God; and you shall love your God with all your heart, with all your soul and all your might.* — Deuteronomy 6:4

To this Jesus may well have added Leviticus 19:18:, "... and thy neighbor as thyself," as he did in response to the Pharisee's question, "Which commandment in the law is the greatest?" (Matthew 22:36-39) This, in itself, would have been a clue to the Emmaus travelers that they were speaking to none other than the Master, himself.

After the *Shema,* Jesus might well have added some verses from one of the Psalms, such as this passage from Psalm 103:

Bless the Lord, O my soul, and all that is within me, bless his holy name. Bless the Lord, O my soul, and forget not his benefits.

or, from Psalm 104:

O Lord my God, you are very great . . . you bring forth food from the earth, and wine to gladden the human heart, oil to make the face shine, and bread to strengthen the human heart.

Very likely, to these traditional words, Jesus would have added words of his own, addressing God in a very characteristic way as Abba, to which the nearest English equivalent is Papa!

Abba, I thank you that you have given eternal life to all whom you have entrusted to me. All mine are yours, and yours are mine. Protect in your name, Abba, those whom you have given me, so that they may be one, as we are one. Amen.

If our imagined reconstruction is anywhere near the mark, we can understand why those Emmaus travelers' "eyes were opened and they recognized him." (Luke 24:31) Along with characteristic gestures that Luke does not describe was Jesus' utterly unique and unprecedented way of addressing God: Abba!

Such a plausible table grace as that above underscores three characteristics of Jesus' devotional life which provide an important model for Christians today. Part one, the *Shema*, reminds the pray-er of the divine primacy of the one God of covenant history. Part two, the Psalm portion, connects us to the worshiping community of God's faithful people past and present, and reminds us to whom we and the earth belong. The third part, a very personal prayer to a very personal God, relates us to the God of grace who "marks the sparrow's fall" (Luke 12:6) and, like a good shepherd, "knows his sheep." (John 10:14)

The Lord's Prayer (Matthew 6:10) provides the same model: beginning with the grandeur of God and the promised kingdom, continuing with the provider of daily bread, and concluding with the gracious God who hears our confessions of shortcomings and delivers us from evil.

The Last Supper most certainly began with a table prayer like the one we have suggested above. Because of that Supper's proximity to the Passover, Jesus may well have used for the Psalm portion one of the review-of-covenant-history psalms, like Psalm 105, including:

Remember the wonderful works [the Lord] has done ... he remembered his holy promise, and Abraham his servant. He brought his people out with joy, his chosen ones with singing ... He gave them food from heaven in abundance. He gave them a land flowing with milk and honey that they might be his people and he their God. Praise the Lord!

We don't have to guess what were the personal aspects of the evening's prayers. John provides us with a poignant intercessory prayer in chapter 17. In an hour in which we would have understood if Jesus had been preoccupied with his imminent betrayal and arrest, he is, instead, concerned about his disciples — their safety, (v. 15) their unity, (v. 11) their perseverance, (v. 17) their endurance under persecution, their sense of being commissioned to spread the truth of the gospel, (vv. 18 and 20) and their persistence in love. (v. 26)

Such a prayer in the disciples' presence is most fitting after the table talk which Jesus gives. (John 14-16) The fracturing of their unity had already begun in the argument over greatness at that same table, (Luke 22:24) the exposure of Judas' disloyalty and the prediction of Peter's denial (Luke 22:33-34) — an alarming prelude to their greatest testing only a few hours away! Jesus reassures them that he will never stop being an empowering presence for them, as a vine to its branches, "Abide in me, as I abide in you," he said. (John 15:4)

If they perceive him as one who is laying down his life for his friends, then they must love one another as he has loved them. (John 15:13)

The great promise of this table talk is that of the advocate, the Holy Spirit. The spirit of truth, like Jesus, comes from the Father and will prove Christ's detractors wrong, (16:8) guide Christians into all the truth, (v. 13) and glorify Christ. (v. 14) "Take courage," Jesus concludes, "I have conquered the world!" (v. 33)

No words could have been more sensitive to the disciple's needs in that moment. There was only one thing left for Jesus to do to seize the moment even further. He asked them to join him in prayer again, as they had at the beginning of the meal. That is the marvelous prayer that John reconstructs for us in chapter 17, a prayer of joyful anticipation of victory through suffering, confidence of completed work, trust in God, commitment of his friends to the care of the Father, petition for their unity, safety and ensuing mission.

Even better, as John presents it, it is the only place where Jesus is pictured praying for you and me! "... not for these only, but also for all those who will believe in me through their word, that they may all be one." (17:20-21)

It is tragically ironic that Christ's prayer for oneness among his followers present and future should have come at the Last Supper. Tragic because a sacrament that was meant to unite us has often been practiced in ways that expose our disunity. After nearly 20 centuries a proposal has come for mutual recognition of ministries. And the decades of old Consultation on Church Union's proposal for covenanting relationships among its participating churches is meeting very mixed reactions from clergy of every persuasion. Despite assurances from members of the Consultation that clergy will not be ordained or reordained to oversee the Church of Christ Uniting, protectionist arguments proliferate. Who cannot hear the disciples quibbling over "which one of them was to be regarded as the greatest." (Luke 22:24)

We need to look again at the prayers at the Supper. Together with other participating churches, we now have the possibility to start the pilgrimage that could be, by the 21st century, begin to embody more visibly the unity for which our Lord prayed "so that the world might believe." (John 17:21)

One more observation: if prayer was such an important part of Jesus' life, why should it not be an important part of our lives? It was a continuing battle for Jesus to convince his friends that they could not expect to cope or witness without giving a significant place to prayer in their daily lives. When they were powerless to help an epileptic boy, Jesus said it was because they did not pray. (Mark 9:29) When in those critical moments before his arrest, he asked them to lend their prayer power to his, they fell asleep. (Mark 14:37) So the Bible is realistic about the human tendency to see prayer as something for formal occasions, a panic button in times of crises or an habitual practice with little emotional content.

But the Bible is clear, as well, on the power that came to Jesus only by prayer. Forced many times to abandon his balance of prayer and mission, Jesus is pictured again and again pushing through the crowds to a place apart for the renewal that only prayer could give, even if it meant getting in a boat and rowing to the other side of a lake! A major part of the Sermon on the Mount is Jesus' teaching regarding prayer. He is aware of prayer for show, (Matthew 6:5), but he is also aware of prayer that is primarily between you and God. ("in secret" v. 6) That God rewards such prayer is Jesus' promise.

Therein lies the secret to a vital prayer life. Not that it knows certain techniques or is an obligation, but that it knows to whom it prays! Jesus understood his improverishment if he did not have dialogue with his Abba. Once we understand that God is a loving parent who is on our side, missed opportunities for prayer are like missed opportunities to eat or sleep, to bathe or to breathe. To have one's own prayers joined by those of others fortifies us for many tests and challenges, perhaps even Gethsemanes and Golgothas. So it is with Jesus and, ultimately, with the disciples. So it will be for us.

Pentecost

A MEAL FOR THE ROAD

Eating with others — often a very casual exercise in our culture: fast food, grabbed food, snack on the run; business lunches, fuel stops, shopping breaks, brown bags at desks. For many couples and families, it is rare to sit down together and eat and converse in an unhurried manner — meals where there is food for the soul as well as the body. Spouses and children sometimes wonder if they are married to a newspaper or a television. Music blares loudly from the radio. It is a rare situation indeed, where intimate associates make significant visual and verbal contact across a meal table. We eat with loved ones as if they were strangers and strangers as if they were not present. We masticate our food equally well with competitors, enemies, and "what's 'is names."

How different it was for biblical people. To eat with someone, break bread with another, had far more significance than it has in our own day and culture. It implied the sealing of a friendship, a promise of loyalty, and the making of a covenant. One did not eat, then, with an enemy or an adversary. So, perhaps we get an insight into why the Pharisees were generally critical of Jesus because he ate, they said, "with sinners and publicans," (Matthew 9:11), implying that he accepted them as equals, even as friends.

In addition, the Jewish people could not forget the meals that God had provided at strategic points in their historic pilgrimage as a people, chiefly the Passover — that meal of unleavened bread, bitter herbs and roast lamb, recalling the hasty departure from Egyptian slavery, and the saving lamb's blood on the door sills. But there was also the meal of manna and quail — bread and meat coming miraculously at their time of great need in the wilderness sojourn. There was also the meal of biscuits that God provided through the widow of Zarephath for traveler Elijah during a famine. Her meal jar and oil cruse were never to be empty again: meals, miraculous meals by which God's traveling people were nourished and blessed.

It takes place at the next to last stop of Jesus' Passover pilgrimage. Soon he would walk to Gethsemane, then to Pilate's and Herod's Jerusalem quarters, and finally to Golgotha, the Hill of the Skulls. The room was borrowed, as was the cup and the plate, the towel and the basin. There, at that simple table, the bread and the wine, plain Jewish fare, were miraculously enabled to convey the body and the blood of Christ — the energy of his life given for his followers.

Jesus didn't allow his friends to sit around continuing to casually sip wine, eat grapes, and swap stories, as might usually be expected to happen after non-traveling friends sup together. He invited them to stand with him, sing a psalm, and stride down the hill with him, across the Kidron Valley to a garden called Gethsemane.

With us, when communion takes place in the same way each time, in the same setting, with the same shiny silver appointments on white linen, it is easy for us to lose sight of the fact that the first meal was hastily improvised, using borrowed space and borrowed instruments. Someone has commented that children may grow up thinking that Jesus was crucified on white linen between two candles, instead of on a cross between two thieves. I am concerned that regular partakers of communion may carry the impression that the Last Supper was a formal ritual instead of a climactic meal for the road!

It is becoming clear to me that the Lord's Supper, like the first Passover meal, like the feast of manna and quail, and like Elijah's meal of fried cakes, was a meal for travelers — indeed, a meal for the road. Jesus' followers were at the beginning of theirs — a new road; one that would lead to Pentecost, into every province of the Roman Empire, through fierce Roman persecution; later, to the mixed blessing of imperial recognition, and finally into the expanding world!

Like all travelers, these travelers would need food to sustain them — food unlike that which the world could offer, a spiritual food from the still available and still living Lord himself; food that rejuvenates, calms and reassures. By this meal, Jesus said, his followers would remember him and his promises.

And what are those promises? There are three of them that are prominent: "I will drink this wine new with you in my Father's house," (Matthew 26:29) "I will enable you to love one another as I have loved you," (John 13:34, author's paraphrase) and "Lo, I am with you always, even to the end of the age." (Matthew 28:20)

The people of God are travelers again. We are challenged to move beyond our parochial concepts of favored-nation-church; to call to account a culture which assumes it has a divine right to pillage the earth and to pursue economic advantage over other people of God's world. We must challenge our people to move from the concept of the world as our "oyster" to an image of the world as our body, an appendage of ourselves. We are charged to move from seeking comfort for ourselves to seeking comfort for the rest of God's children, in Christ's name and in his spirit. We are called to move from apathy to empathy, from condoning to cajoling, from existing to living, from using to loving. And we are being called to move from relating to other people as "passing ships in the night" to relating as I to thou, in dialogue, with empathy, in mutual support and concern, with respect and compassion.

I do not know what happens when this meal is received each time as if it were not food for travelers but food for the pious indolent, the apathetic. I cannot help but wonder if this is one of those "unworthy" partakings to which Paul alluded in 1 Corinthians 11:27. I do know that Christ is ready to give calm and comfort where that is needed. But he is never a sustainer for the apathetic or uninvolved.

I remember that right after that Upper Room meal Jesus was disappointed when he was agonizing and struggling over God's course for his life in the hours immediately ahead. "Could you not watch with me one brief hour?" he asked the three disciples he'd invited to accompany him. (Matthew 26:40) He thought that he had communicated to them the urgency and seriousness of this fork in his road. Their meal together had been for him a meal for the journey, as it should have been for them — and as it should be for us.

I recall another blessed meal, as recorded by Luke. It was another meal for the road. There they were, oblivious to the resurrection of Jesus — two followers on the road to Emmaus: weary, despairing over the sudden, tragic, violent end to their hopes and dreams, with the execution of their Master.

It is when the Sojourner who had joined them on the road breaks bread with them in a wayside inn that they recognize who he is. Luke says that they commenced their journey then with their hearts "burning within them." (Luke 24:32)

My prayer for Christians today is that after truly partaking of the Lord's Supper as a meal for the road, they will depart with their hearts burning within them.

Pentecost

PEOPLE CHANGE WITH JESUS AT THE TABLE

Playwrights have had fun this last half-century with plots that thicken when someone unusual comes to dinner. There was *The Man Who Came To Dinner*, about the acidly sarcastic dinner guest with the massive ego who broke his leg before leaving and, to the chagrin of his unsuspecting hosts, set up office in their home, expecting everyone to cater to his slightest whim. Later came the provocative movie, *Guess Who's Coming To Dinner?* which featured a situation where a daughter surprised her parents when she invited her black boyfriend home for dinner. Her upper-crust parents' attempts to conceal their shock and disorientation as the guest defied their stereotypes left us amused and embarrassed. We were forced to examine our own stereotypes!

The Bible is full of dinners that changed people, starting with Jacob disguised as his brother Esau, bringing the savory food and bread and stealing Esau's birthright in the process. Things would never be the same for any of them. Then there was the feast of Nebuchadnezzar and the unseen guest's "handwriting on the wall." (Daniel 5:5)

Life-changing dinners in the New Testament are invariably associated with Jesus. Aware that, in that culture's tradition, breaking bread with another was a sign of acceptance and often of commitment to a relationship or an agreement, Jesus used dinner occasions to demonstrate God's valuing everyone and to confront self-righteous people with their prejudices.

I want to recall just two of them today and how two outcast people were changed when Jesus was at the table.

Zacchaeus was outcast because he was a tax collector for the colonial task-masters. His salary was gleaned from whatever "commission" he cared to charge. His people saw him as a traitor and a robber. His curiosity about Jesus who had called a tax collector to be a disciple caused him to risk anger and ridicule by climbing into a tree to see Jesus from a better vantage-point.

We don't know what his expectations were. We can assume that Zacchaeus was friendless, even excluded from the synagogue where he might have spiritual surfeit. Jesus might have been, in a sense, his last chance to see if there was a possibility for friendship human or divine.

You know the story, Jesus' eyes were instinctively drawn to the figure in the tree. He picked up Zacchaeus' name from the jeers of the crowd as they shook their fists at him. At first, perhaps, Zacchaeus thought Jesus was joining in the ridicule but, no, Jesus was urging him to come down and prepare to have him as a house guest, "I must stay at your house today." That brought irritated mumblings from the crowd, of course, but Zacchaeus was oblivious to everything but the fact that Jesus wanted to come to his — yes, his — house for dinner. "So he made haste," writes Luke, "jumped down and received Jesus joyfully." (Luke 19:6)

You see, to have Jesus, this man of God beyond peer, accept him like that was tantamount to receiving the forgiveness of God. "He received Jesus joyfully." That's what God looks for — that we receive His Son joyfully. Things begin to change from the moment we do that. And so it was with Zacchaeus.

With incredulous neighbors peeking through the windows, shaking their heads that Jesus would go "to be the guest of a man who is a sinner," Zacchaeus took a morsel of bread, held it in his hand and announced, "Behold, Lord, the half of my worth I give to the poor; and if I have defrauded anyone of anything, I restore it four-fold." Then he ate the bread and passed back a piece to Jesus, the sealing of a pact! It couldn't have been a more solid commitment had there been 20 notaries present! And Jesus was overjoyed, "Today salvation has come to this house and Zacchaeus is part of the family of Abraham again! Truly, this is my mission, to seek and to save the lost." That last exclamation was not for Zacchaeus' benefit but for that of the cocked ears straining at the door and windows.

Making restitution over and above what might ordinarily be expected was Zacchaeus' way of repenting. No one had to tell him that his questionable vocation had alienated his neighbors. Having found in Jesus' response to him what acceptance can mean, Zacchaeus took the giant step to be reconciled to his neighbors as well as to God. There he stood: a man transformed by Jesus at his table. When Jesus chose to eat with him, Zacchaeus understood it to be God's invitation to redemption, and he could call Jesus by no other name than "Lord!"

Another outcast who was changed with Jesus at the table was the anonymous "woman of the city" (a euphemism for "street walker"). Tradition has assumed that this was Mary Magdalene. At any rate, the Pharisee-host recognized her as a local prostitute, and discounted her as "a sinner." (Luke 7:39)

She had probably been watching Jesus from a discreet distance for some time. No doubt his unusual acceptance of common people especially caught her attention. But even as she was drawn to him by his tolerance, she was put off by her own unworthiness. How could it really be expected that this good rabbi would not be repulsed and shocked by what she had done to survive? Getting up the courage to approach him had been an agonizing process for her.

But for this moment the crowds were gone and Jesus had stepped into a Pharisee's house for dinner, probably a courtyard partly open to the street. She had, perhaps, watched and noticed that the Pharisee host had failed to provide for the washing of his guest's feet. I picture her running to her hovel and drawing from its hiding place the only thing of value that she owned: an alabaster flask of ointment given to her when a girl by her mother for use on her wedding day. Breathless, she entered and knelt just behind him where he was reclining on a cushion at the low table.

Finding herself this close to this good and compassionate man caused feelings of unworthiness and gratitude to well up in her, and the tears came, not in drops but in torrents that she worked frantically to wipe away. The costly ointment came in a flood, as well, lovingly worked into Jesus' road-sore feet. Seeing that he did not pull away from this humble service, she found herself kissing his feet, also, much as a mother might kiss the feet of a child she was bathing.

You know the rest of the story. The Pharisee-host acted as predictably as this rabbi from Nazareth did unpredictably. And, in that moment Jesus longed for there to be another changed person as he sat at table, so he tried to point out to his host what was happening: "She did the courtesy that you failed to do; she weeps out of regret for the life she has lived, and the forgiveness she hoped to find here has been realized. She has done what God longs for every child to do; and I can say to her now, 'Go in peace; your faith is not in vain.' Will you be one who is forgiven little because he loves little, or will you remember the lesson of the tears and the ointment?"

As in so many gospel accounts, we are left with the question. We don't know if the Pharisee was forced to look in upon himself, to see that even a woman of the streets can teach a learned and self-righteous Pharisee some important lessons.

Dare I say that Jesus was changed at this supper also, by the woman's act of service? Did memories of her washing his feet — the tears and the ointment — come back to him as he searched that night before the Passover for some way to dramatize to the disciples, so drawn in upon themselves, what loving service is about?

For at that supper table, also, no one assumed the role of the servant: the washing of the guests' feet. Did the vivid recollection of the woman washing his feet the way she did come back to Jesus as he seized the opportunity the moment offered, filled a basin with water, wrapped a towel around his waist, and commenced to wash the feet of his flustered companions? He set the stage for explicit statement of a commandment that he had implied in his words to the Pharisee, "He who loves little is forgiven little:" "You must love one another as I have loved you." (John 13:34)

John attaches so much importance to this incident, that he makes foot-washing, not communion, the second sacrament! It said to him that in relationships there is, in the final analysis, only one virtue that really matters: love! And the source of that love is the God who serves. "Little children, love one another. He who loves is born of God and knows God, for God is love." (1 John 4:7)

When you come to his table, Jesus wants it to be a time for positive change, as it was for Zacchaeus, for the woman, hopefully for the Pharisee and for the disciples. This is where the food is. This is the gate of heaven. Sense his presence here, respond to it in your hungry heart, and you may be changed, too.

Thanksgiving

SINGING PSALMS OF THANKSGIVING

From sorrow to thanksgiving: that is the emotional transition at the Last Supper, as Matthew and Mark picture it. "They began to be sorrowful ..." (Mark 14:19a) as Jesus shared with them the fact that one of them was planning to betray him. Peter's recollection, as shared with Mark, is that rather than look accusingly at one another, each of the 12 looked inwardly, understood his own potential for disloyalty and, in turn asked, "Is it I, Lord?" (Mark 14:19)

That is a remarkable response from those who had been arguing earlier (Mark 9:34) about which of them would be greatest. Here at Jesus' table, where the Master has assumed the menial task of washing feet when no one else would come forward (John 13:5-11) and spoken of imminent betrayal on the road to a cross, it was impossible to think of one's own reward and recognition. Only three words would do: "Is it I?" — words uttered "sorrowfully," as Peter recalls.

How moving it is, then, to read that at the end of this emotionally racking hour they sang Psalms of Thanksgiving. Mark specifically tells us, "After the Psalms had been sung ..." (14:26, NJB) If ever there was a reason not to "close the meeting with singspiration," this was surely it! What is there to sing about? Jesus humiliated us with a servant act of washing feet, predicted his betrayal at the hands of one of us, and told us that this is our last meal with him. Now he asks us to sing praises to God, Psalms of gratitude to God; to join voices in thanksgiving to God!

But, wait a minute, there were some magnificent promises in his acts and words here, as well. The sharing of this body and blood in the bread and the wine, so like the Passover but significantly new and different, had "sealed" his word of promise, "...I [will] drink it new [with you] in the kingdom of God." (Mark 14:25)

That glorious promise can move us to thanksgiving and overshadow the themes of betrayal and separation!

The singing of Psalms at the close of that time together had several significant effects. For those who were still red of face for demurring from the servant act of footwashing, or still turned inward at the thought of betrayal potential, or hot with anger toward Judas, or anxious at the prospect of the dangerous hours ahead, the singing of the Psalms of Israel would have a healing result. The singing of the Psalms is a corporate act, reuniting me with the extended family, the people of God, the covenant people of which I am a part. It lifts me from self-preoccupation and focuses us all on the mercies of our God and Father. There is something and someone larger than my own shame or my own ambition — a gracious Creator-God who counts me worthy to be a part of God's redemptive plan for all of the world. That kingdom promise, that kingdom hope, is truly something to be thankful about!

And I think we can assume that, as for them, the singing of Psalms of thanksgiving was rejuvenating for Jesus as well. Travel through the gospels and see at what significant points Jesus recalled the songs of his people's faith. Start with the beginning of his walk with the disciples, as he articulated the guiding principles of the breaking-in kingdom, the Beatitudes and the Sermon on the Mount:

The meek shall inherit the earth.
— Psalm 37:11a

Those who sow in tears shall reap with shouts of joy.
— Psalm 126:5

Who shall ... stand in God's holy presence? They that have ... a pure heart. — Psalm 24:3-4

It is in vain that you go late to rest, eating the bread of anxious toil, for God gives rest to his beloved.
— Psalm 127:2

Continue with numerous images drawn from the Psalms and permeating his teachings on hillsides, lakeshores and byways. The value of using Psalm language and pictures in his public teaching cannot be overestimated. His creativity, incorporating those phrases and images into fresh and vivid teaching, made the common people sure that this voice was echoing and reverberating from the same divine light. "He teaches not as our scribes but as one with authority" they exclaimed in amazement." (Mark 1:22)

And in those moments of greatest testing and agony, as he hung on the cross, Jesus returned to the Psalms for affirmation, comfort and reassurance: (Luke 23:46; Matthew 27:46)

Into your hand I commit my spirit ...
— Psalm 31:5a

My God, my God, why have you forsaken me?
— Psalm 22:1

The moment we understand that Jesus, in the hour of his most profound suffering service, was drawing on the Psalms for strength, comfort and resolve, these words from the cross lose any oppressive overtones. For Psalms 31 and 32 are not songs of despair but of thanksgiving and victory! Read on and see:

Into your hands I commit my spirit; you have redeemed me, O Lord, faithful God.

My God, my God, why have you forsaken me? ... Yet in you our ancestors trusted ... and you delivered them ... it was you who took me from my mother's womb and kept me safe on my mother's breast ... and since my mother bore me you have been my God ... [now] many bulls encircle me ... they open wide their mouths ...raving and roaring lions. I am poured out like water ... my heart is melted within my breast... From the horns of the wild oxen you have rescued me. I will tell of your name to my kindred: God did not hide his face from me, but heard when I cried to him! ... Future generations will be told about the Lord, and proclaim his deliverance to a people yet unborn!

To his Roman executioners, the soldiers standing 'round, the first few audible words could only be interpreted as words of dereliction, but to those for whom the Psalms had been their worship-book, the hymnbook of triumph and defeat over generations of growing into covenant identity, it could be a sign of thankful and resilient faith!

There in the Upper Room, as darkness fell, Jesus, too, needed to have the spiritual reinforcement that the old hymnbook of his people could arouse. He looked, in vain, for encouragement in the faces around him. What he saw was only confusion, sadness and fear. So he did what was, apparently, most natural for him to do, he began the chants of his people, songs of thanks to God, recounting God's blessings from their past and taking hold of God's sure promises for their future.

Why might Jesus have come to the end of that Upper Room time depleted in spiritual energy? Ask that of anyone who is continually on the "giving end" of succorance. In one place, at least, the account is very clear about the expendability of Jesus' caring resources. In the healing of the hemorrhaging woman who touched him in the pressing crowd, Jesus, says

Mark, "immediately sensed that power had gone forth from him." (Mark 5:30a)

Perhaps Jesus had come to that Supper seeking for himself, as well as for the disciples, renewed power, fresh clarity about the course he had taken, and the reassurance of those who understand. If that depended upon the disciples, there would have been mainly disappointment. One had already conspired with the priests against Jesus; none of them chose to volunteer to wash the other's feet, as religion and etiquette required; none of them shared his understanding of suffering messiahship; and Peter made hollow promises about loyalty to the end.

No, if Jesus had depended upon the disciples to provide confirmation about his messianic mission, human reassurance and prayerful support, he would have been disappointed, indeed. He had to draw from deeper wells, and one of them was the Psalms of thanks and faith. He led them in singing the Psalms:

A table thou hast furnished
In presence of my foes;
My head thou dost with oil anoint,
And my cup overflows.

Goodness and mercy all my life
Shall surely follow me;
And in God's house forever more
My dwelling place shall be.

He had in the Supper that night provided a thanksgiving feast for his friends. Now God was providing a spiritual feast for him!

Soprano Sun Sook Lee testifies to the power of faith-music to heal, restore and give reassurance as she travels the country's churches offering a musical autobiography. It is a moving account of how, having almost lost her childhood faith amidst the glamour of operatic success, she was brought back by her mother's fatal stroke. Rushing back home to Korea to be at her unconscious mother's bedside, she found that the only words she could summon beyond, "I love you, Mom. Forgive me if I have hurt you in any way," were the hymns her mother had sung to her. There was no certainty that her mother heard her, but the hymns became God's word to Sun Sook as she resolved to abruptly end her highly celebrated operatic career and devote herself to Christian recitals. Well-known organist-producer Diane Bish became interested, and Sun Sook's musical ministry was launched, a ministry which she pursues radiantly, to this day! She ends every recital with Handel's "Thanks be to Thee."

Don't misunderstand. It is the Supper that transforms us, as it would for the disciples in the years ahead. But on that evening, as the darkness indeed descended, the singing of their people's Psalms of Thanksgiving had its encouraging, reassuring and faith-strengthening effect, as it does for us, and as it will for those to follow us. We, too, may move from sorrow to singing if we remember to sing songs of thanksgiving to God!

Confirmation or New Year's Sunday

WHAT WE BRING AND WHAT WE RECEIVE

Perhaps those to be confirmed today remember Dickens' *A Christmas Carol*? Scrooge is confronted by ghosts of his past, future and present. The morose specter of his past reveals that he carries guilt as a web of chains and padlocks weighing him down. The gruesome specter of his future reveals his fear that he will perish unnoticed, with nothing but the cold wind to sigh at his grave. The vision of his present has him enviously watching the happy relationships in Bob Cratchet's home; a home poor in things but rich in love. It comes to Scrooge that all he has earned for himself through the years of penny-pinching is regret over the past, fear for the future and lovelessness in the present.

Each Christmas we find ourselves fixated on this story, not simply because of Dickens' masterful characterizations, but because too often it speaks of our experience. We know what it is to live in the past by guilt, in the future by anxiety, and in the present as those who are unable to be present for others.

Three "words" at the Supper speak to our predicament:

This cup is the new covenant sealed in my blood. Do this, as often as you drink it, in remembrance of me.
— 1 Corinthians 11:25-26

I will not drink again of the fruit of the vine until I drink it new with you in my Father's kingdom.
— Matthew 26:29

Those who love me ... my Father will love ... and we will make our home with them. — John 14:25

Just as I have loved you, you also should love one another. — John 14:34

These great words give confirmands the key to living in the past by faithful remembrance, in the future by confident hope and in the present by love.

Emil Brunner, the late Swiss theologian was the first to have the insight that Paul's trilogy — faith, hope and love — speak to our past, future and present human dilemma. He said in those 1955 Earl Lectures, that faith has to do with the basis, the ground on which we stand; hope is reaching out for something to come; and love is just being there and acting.

Jesus understood that the disciples, gathered around that table that night, represented a microcosm of the human condition. He had walked in their shoes before he called them. The temptation in the wilderness was simply a summary experience of numerous experiences Jesus had of human tornness. The awareness that was his as he sat down at that table, "knowing that the Father had given all things into his hands, and that he had come from God and was going to God ..." (John 13:3) was not arrived at overnight. His full human identification with us made him subject to all the temptations and misgivings that we have experienced. (see Hebrews 4:15)

The disciples' reaction, with one voice, "Is it I, Lord?" to Jesus' prediction that one of them would betray him, and Peter's reaction when Jesus moved to him with the basin and towel, "... not my feet only, Lord, but also my hands and my head!" (John 13:9) are ample clues to their feelings of guilt over their past. And which of us cannot identify with that in terms of our failures in the past about where our heads, our hands and our feet have been!

"If only" becomes a common signature phrase for some: If only I had shown that person I loved them; if only I had persevered and developed that gift, hung in that relationship, hadn't been so proud, so vengeful, so lustful, so impulsive, so foolish, so self-righteous or so temperamental!

We are conscious, too, of corporate guilt; the fact that we were part of a perverse and erring society. I was apathetic when all that cruelty or unfairness was going on. I did nothing to call my family, my neighbors, my people to a higher humanity. Created to love people and use things, more often than not I have, like others, loved things and used people.

This pummeling of ourselves for what we did or failed to do in the past, no matter how warranted, takes a lot of energy and attention away from the possibilities of the present.

To those being confirmed Jesus says, "Remember me. My redemptive work in your behalf can transport you from guilt for your past to salvation. There is no need to go from this room carrying regrets, like an albatross, into the present and the future. I go to a cross so that you may leave your sins there." The cross liberates us from guilt over our past. We have but to remember him.

The second word of Jesus that speaks to humanity's "triple bind" is a word about the future: "I will . . . drink of the fruit of the vine with you in my Father's kingdom." Paul underscores this promise when he writes, "For as often as we eat this bread and drink this cup, we proclaim the Lord's death until he comes." (1 Corinthians 11:26) That says to you that he who invites you to this table and is present now by the Holy Spirit, will one day be manifest in a new form as the undisputed Savior of the world. This meal is not the kingdom, the victory feast. It is the appetizer, the dress rehearsal, the precursor. The feast with God and "all the saints" is yet to be experienced and this precious meal is the guarantee! The promise, like the new covenant, is sealed in this meal.

Christians may approach their future with hope instead of fear because of Jesus' promise that he will eat and drink with us in his Father's kingdom. I can anticipate the future with hope, not anxiety, because I have God's assurance that I will experience Christ as the undisputed conqueror of hearts and wills, the victorious Lord of history!

The love that we have known in Jesus will win out totally over any other claims upon our devotion, and will triumph over our perversity and inconsistency "There is no limit to love's endurance, no fading of its hope, it can outlast anything!" (1 Corinthians 13:7 JBP)

To your anxiety over the future the Host of this table lifts the glass and proposes a toast, "To me and you, in my Father's kingdom!"

Not only do I bring my guilt over the past and my fear of the future to this table for transformation, but I bring my lovelessness in the present.

Love in the New Testament is different from the confusing kaleidoscope practiced and sold to you by our warped society. The love of 1 Corinthians 13 is not an affection I feel for someone because they're admirable or desirable. Neither is it those investments I've made in a relationship in anticipation of some kind of "pay off." Christ's love is best defined as uncalculating love. It's origin is not with me but with the love of God. If I can love unselfishly now, even for a moment, it is only because the One who "makes his sun to shine on the just and the unjust" motivates me to do so. My love has too often been one which comes with needs. Agape comes with gifts.

The word the Host of the table has for you and your paralysis in the present is, "Love as I have loved you." Jesus frees you from guilt over the past and fear for the future so that you can be present for others, open to their needs, free to be with them wholeheartedly, perceiving their beauty and uniqueness. Because Jesus said, "Remember, I am here for you," you can say that to others from the heart!

Without Jesus' love, we are seldom really present for other people. We are so preoccupied with our own past and our own future, we are shut up, enclosed within ourselves. But Christ has said to us, "Suffer no more over that, remember me. I have dealt with your past; I have dealt with your guilt. Let it stay buried under the cross." That is what redemption and reconciliation are all about. And now Christ makes us free from our future as anxiety by saying, "Together, all of us, in my Father's kingdom!" Now we are being formed into those who love. Glad recipients of God's forgiveness, we are confident that we are being molded into a channel of God's love.

God makes us sheep into co-shepherds. (See John 21:15-17) "Love one another as I have loved you," Jesus says. We can't be touched by God's love without being set afire by the same flames. God won't settle for us merely admiring unconditional love, God shares agape with us, enabling us to participate in it.

This is the bread that Jesus gives to confirmands at this table. The bread that we bring is our guilt, our anxiety, and our lovelessness. The bread he gives is forgiveness, hope and love, and he gives it with his body and his blood. It is in his offering of these that our suffering may be made sacred.

As in all fellowship, here in the Lord's Supper, the giving and receiving move both ways. By receiving this bread and wine you take into your lives the nurture and healing of God. And by forgiveness God takes your sufferings upon God's self so that God is present in the very midst of them.

Christian faith, then, at these points of past, future and present, is never a running away. It is a coming forward. We bring an offering and we receive an offering. In the words of the late David E. Roberts:

> *We bring a broken world, a broken humanity, broken selves. In return we receive broken bread. And by the transforming presence of Christ, that which was broken*

is made whole again. *What is received is a sacramental universe, time tied together, true community, and redemption.*[1]

---

[1] *The Grandeur and Misery of Man* (Oxford University Press, 1955), p. 117.

First Communion

A NEW MEAL FOR A NEW COVENANT

Those observing their first communion should know that the Last Supper is better called the First Supper! "Now on the first day of unleavened bread the disciples came to Jesus saying, 'Where will you have us eat the Passover?' " (Matthew 26:17) Some understand the Last Supper to be tacked on to a Seder or Passover celebration. John takes exception. He makes a good case for calling communion the First Supper: "Now before the feast of the Passover, when Jesus knew his time was running out, he rose from supper, girded himself with a towel and began to wash the disciples' feet." (John 13:3-5)

Why does John contradict the other record? What point is he trying to make by disassociating the Lord's Supper from the old Passover?

It is generally agreed that John's gospel was written later than the others and that though it displays more freedom in interpreting Jesus' teachings, paraphrasing and even adding to what Jesus had said, it is by far the most perceptive in catching the spirit of Jesus' teachings and, even more importantly, the most telling in terms of what Jesus and his ministry meant for future generations of communicants.

John, like an art lover standing back to view a work from a slight distance lest he miss the total effect from standing too close, scans the life of Jesus and concludes, "The true light that enlightens everyone was coming into the world." (John 1:9)

John, perhaps with Jesus' "You don't put new wine into old wineskins" (Matthew 9:17) ringing in his ears, insists that this is a unique and unprecedented meal that Jesus was instituting, just as the "Love one another" commandment at the end of the meal was new. It was not tacked on to the Seder. What Jesus brought was not to be seen as a revision of something already in place. It was a new sacrament for an entirely new covenant — a new meal for a new age. This new covenant supersedes any previous covenants, and yet itself will never be superseded!

Without a doubt, when John read the account of the other gospels about how Jesus said, "This is the cup of the new covenant sealed in my blood." (1 Corinthians 11:25) he recalled Jeremiah 31:31 about a new covenant:

> *Behold, the days are coming, says the Lord, when I will make a new covenant ... not like the covenant which I made with those whom I led out of Egypt, the covenant which they broke, though I was their husband ... but this is a new covenant I will make: I will put my law within them, will write it upon their hearts, and I will be their God and they shall be my people. No longer shall each one teach his neighbor and kin saying "Know the Lord," for they shall all know me, from the least of them to the greatest ... for I will forgive their iniquity and remember their sin no more.* — Jeremiah 31:31-34

John knew that a brand new covenant demanded a brand new meal, and so he carefully disassociated the Lord's Supper from an observance of a Seder. He let the Synoptic Gospels' account of the "cup of the new covenant" and the bread of the broken body of Christ stand, offering no new words of institution, as we say, but he added the foot washing and the New Commandment. Why?

Because John wanted to go farther than Jeremiah, who, inspired as he was, could only have guessed what God's ultimate objective might be — in abrogating the former covenant and instituting a new and better one. The former covenant was designed for toddlers — those who must be "led by the hand." (Jeremiah 31:32) The later covenant is designed for the growing faithful, those who will gladly present their hearts for tablets, their minds for light, and their very souls to receive and reflect God's grace. Then, and only then, will those observing their first or their hundredth communion be prepared to do what God has longed to see his children do from the beginning of creation: serve and love one another!

Our very discomfort with John's implication that foot washing should be a sacred rite of the new covenant people is, perhaps, an indication of how far we have yet to go to obey the highest and best commandment. "Love one another as I have loved you." (John 13:34) — the verse I would give you on your first communion.

Jeremiah stopped short of a community where love reigns as God's objective and the universe's ultimate destiny. His vision is remarkably advanced, given the depressing historical circumstance from which he spoke at the beginning of the Exile. It is the Prophet of Lamentations' most hopeful vision: people with the ethics of God's kingdom implanted in their hearts, content to be God's loyal people — inspired in their communications, living in the reality and consequence of God's grace, with every vestige of wavering faith dispelled!

But John went even farther and became explicit about the "law written on their hearts." He reflected on the teachings of Jesus and their impact, and asked, "How is this still living Savior's presence manifest to me," And only one word came persistently to mind? Agape! It was the agape of God that caused God to make everything that was made. It was agape that moved God to enter the human arena as a brother and Savior. And it is agape that sustains communicants now and beckons them "beyond the camp." (Hebrews 13:13) In the beginning was agape, and agape became flesh and dwelt among us full of grace and truth. (John 1:14)

It is only logical that in his old age, writing his first epistle, John should have come to the simple and penultimate conclusion: God is love. "Little children, love one another, for love is of God. By our love others know that we are born of God and know God. For God is love." (1 John 4:7-8)

How does that love look in practice? John could well have been speaking to first communicants when he described agape love. Such love, he said, does not become enamored with the world, has no room for hatred, does not close its heart against a brother or sister in need, is not satisfied just to talk about love but seeks to express it in word and deed. It is even prepared to lay down its life for a brother or sister, if love should demand it. (1 John 3:14-18)

The new meal for the new time nourishes communicants for such agape living. It blows air upon the spark of Christ that is within you. It connects you again to the vine from which alone you are nourished. It takes us scattered grains of wheat and makes us into one bread.

The Jewish Seder is rich with significance for the children of Israel. It marked their beginning as a people of God and stood forever as a sign of the liberation from bondage in Egypt. But it could not begin to contain the new powers and the affirmations that emanated from the Upper Room, any more than an old wineskin can contain new wine.

The new time requires a new meal: "For this is my blood of the new covenant," Jesus said. And that is why the Last Supper is really the First; not just yours but the church's, as well.

Questions For Reflection Or Group Discussion

A Meal For The Road

Ruth's Legacy At The Table

1. How is Ruth's commitment to Naomi, half-way through that treacherous journey to Bethlehem, like Jesus' commitment to his disciples on the way to Golgotha?

2. How is Boaz's blessing of Ruth over bread and wine like Jesus' blessing of his disciples over bread and wine? What does Jesus promise?

3. Why does Matthew find room for Ruth, along with Mary, in an otherwise patriarchal genealogy?

Room At The Table

1. What signs at his birth indicated the inhospitality of the world to Jesus?

2. How were the religious leaders particularly inhospitable to Jesus? Why do you think this was so?

3. What was Jesus' response to this inhospitality? What might this say about the nature of God?

4. How is the temptation to judge the "worthiness" of people to receive God's hospitality still present with us?

5. What can we learn from Jesus' response to common people, as well as to his critics?

Crumbs From The Table

1. What compelled the mother of the epileptic girl to ask Jesus to heal her daughter? How is her perseverance demonstrated?

2. Do you think Jesus was right to use the occasion to parody the prejudice of those standing around? How was it a compliment to the woman?

3. How was the widow of Zarephath a model of faith and hope in her response to Elijah's request for bread?

4. What myth about the relationship of suffering and sin did the poor widow reveal when she asked, "Have you come to punish me for some past sin?" How does the story challenge this assumption?

5. The author suggests that the church may need also to examine its ideas of who is in and who is out. Do you agree? Explain.

Foolish Christians

1. Why did Kagawa call himself "a foolish Christian"? Have you ever felt that way?

2. In what ways did Jesus endure being ridiculed and belittled? Why was it important to the gospel writers to record Jesus' experience of ridicule?

3. What characteristics of Christians caused the Gentile world to accuse them of turning the world "upside down"? (Acts 17:6)

4. Does your behavior as a Christian reveal the contrary ways of Jesus?

5. How does an experience of communion help you to endure the costs and risks of conscientious Christian living?

The Gospel In The Supper

1. What aspect of the gospel might be obscured were it not for the frequent reiteration of them at the communion service?

2. Can you think of modern instances where the atonement and suffering servant aspects of the gospel are obscured?

3. What do you think Bonhoeffer meant by "cheap grace"? Why was the fictional character in Paton's novel concerned that he might not have wounds to show?

4. When Paul calls us "joint heirs with Christ, if indeed we suffer with him," what is he telling Christians?

5. What are some of the ways Christ may be calling us to suffering service today?

Judas At The Table

1. Why did Judas become disillusioned with Jesus? What circumstances might cause your faith to waiver?

2. What are the implications for you of Judas' being included at the Table?

3. What does it mean to say "ours is a borrowed righteousness"? What are some ways in which we may be tempted to betray Jesus?

4. When we have "failed" him, how might we find reassurance at the Lord's Supper?

Tangible Signs: Bread And Wine

1. In using common elements, what human need was Jesus recognizing in his followers?

2. In what ways did God respond to the human need for tangible signs with the Hebrew people?

3. Was there merit to the transcendentalist attempt to observe communion without bread and wine? Why did it not take hold?

4. In what way might communion be called "an interim sacrament"? What will ultimately supplant it? What does that prospect mean to you?

Pathos And Celebration In The Supper

1. How does the Lord's Supper express both pathos and celebration?

2. Is it important to preserve both aspects? What would be lost if one or the other were deemphasized?

3. What promise of Jesus' at the Lord's Supper leaves us with a feeling of hope? (see 1 Corinthians 11:26)

Prayer At The Supper

1. How might have Jesus' rendition of the traditional *Shema* been a first clue to the Emmaus travelers that he was their Master?

2. How might Jesus' manner of addressing God as Father been another clue to his identity?

3. What are some of the key themes of Jesus' Last Supper prayer as John relates it in chapter 17?

4. What indication is there in Jesus' prayer that he was including you and me?

5. How today has the Eucharist become too often a sign of our division rather than of our oneness?

6. Do you share the belief that the motivation for a vital prayer life comes more from our understanding of the nature of God than from a sense of duty or knowledge of techniques?

A Meal For The Road

1. What significance did eating together have for biblical people? How can we make our meals more significant?

2. What examples are there of God's providing meals for God's pilgrim people at significant points in their journeying?

3. What meals in your experience have been memorable in a relational and spiritual sense?

4. What did Jesus hope to communicate by transforming that meal the way he did? Are there any indications that he succeeded?

People Change With Jesus At The Table

1. What constituted Zacchaeus' act of repentance?

2. What was it about Jesus that caused Zacchaeus to call him "Lord"? (see Luke 19:1-10)

3. Do you think it was easy for the "woman of the city" to approach Jesus? Explain. (see Luke 7:36-39)

4. In what way might the woman's act have influenced Jesus?

5. What is John's point in making the footwashing a sacrament?

Singing Psalms Of Thanksgiving

1. What was the surprising reaction of the disciples when Jesus announced that one of them would betray him? Do you identify with them? How?

2. Why was singing appropriate or inappropriate after that wrenching time together?

3. Can you think of another time when Jesus found the Psalms a source of encouragement and reassurance?

4. Have you ever used the Psalms in a stressful situation, personally or with another? Explain.

5. Do you feel the renewed interest in singing or chanting Psalms is helpful or regressive? Why?

What We Bring And What We Receive

1. How does Jesus' word, "Remember me" speak to the regret over the past that we bring to the Table?

2. How does Jesus' word, "I will drink it new with you in my Father's kingdom" speak to our anxiety about the future?

3. How does Jesus' word, "Love one another as I have loved you" speak to our distractedness in the present?

4. We bring our "broken bread" to the Table. What does Jesus bring? What difference does it make?

A New Meal For A New Covenant

1. Why did John contradict the other gospel writers about the occasion of the Lord's Supper? What action of Jesus did he alone include?

2. Would there be any value in observing a rite of foot washing today? What might it symbolize for us?

3. What was the "new commandment" of Jesus? How does such love look in practice?

4. How can the whole-hearted and meaningful practice of communion prepare us to show his love?